Making Family Memories

Making Family Memories

Crafts and Activities

Virginia and Rick Ruehlmann

Baker Books

A Division of Baker Book House Co
Grand Rapids, Michigan 49516

© 1994 by Virginia and Rick Ruehlmann

Published by Baker Books
a division of Baker Book House Company
P.O. Box 6287, Grand Rapids, MI 49516-6287

ISBN: 0-8010-7770-2

Second printing, December 1994

Printed in the United States of America

Illustrations by Kathleen Moore and Katherine Lindenschmidt

To all who are
young in age
young at heart
and want to stay
young in spirit

Contents

Contents

Three generations of Ruehlmanns gather for a photo. Four grandchildren missed the occasion. All of them wanted to be included in the book photo because they happily remember doing many of the activities with Grandma Ruehlmann.

Son Rick persuaded his mother to collect her materials and ideas and co-authored this book so other families could also make some unforgettable memories. Rick's suggestion is now reality.

Acknowledgment

Heartfelt appreciation is extended to all the dedicated volunteers, Brownie and Cub Scout and recreation leaders, parents, grandparents, children, granchildren, nieces, nephews, teachers, and friends who through the years have contributed to this book. The compilation of activities has been an ongoing process over the span of many decades. It would be wonderful—and nearly impossible—to attribute the original sources; however, sincere thanks is expressed to all who in some way shaped this collection and thus added to children's learning and enjoyment.

Special recognition is given to Bridget Cornett and to Cheryl Guilfoyle's class 103 of Our Lady of Victory School, Cincinnati, Ohio, for testing the activities to assure the clarity of instructions.

Sincere thanks to the Cincinnati Recreation Commission for the suggested rules for the games of checkers, hopscotch, O'Leary, and jacks.

God bless all who have contributed and all who will benefit from participating in the activities.

Foreword

Some homes you are invited to for a family or social gathering seem rather sterile or formal and the time spent is often awkward and downright boring. Not so when our family of only one child would visit the bustling Ruehlmann home. It was like happily going to camp! The eight Ruehlmann children were extremely happy, bright, energetic, friendly, and *very* active. "Mama Ginny" was always busy cooking and preparing wonderful meals with great ease and tranquility while being able to greet and genuinely inquire of wants and concerns of all guests from toddler to octogenarian.

The home was warm and ambient, mixing beautiful heirlooms with a myriad of projects, either in process or completed, that her children were displaying. Presently the same decorative scheme prevails, but the projects are those of her grandchildren. Before partaking of wonderful cuisine, everyone was engaged in comfortable activity. The children, according to age groups, were welcomed into some activity ranging from volleyball or touch football for the older youth, to children's games or projects for the younger guests. The Ruehlmann kinder magnificently enfolded all youthful guests into the various activities. We older folks were entertained by all the exuberance and energy of the children at their play, as well as our own conversation catching up with all the news about the guests and the Ruehlmann family. Father of the clan, Gene, was always busy providing necessary materials and equipment for all the activity and overseeing all that was happening. He was the city mayor and camp counselor, but Ginny was the camp director!

Perhaps the most boring or uninteresting time during most home social visits is the period of time following a great meal, when the men and women seem obliged to form separate groups to engage in shallow conversation and the children are fidgeting about with nothing much to occupy their interest. Not so at the Ruehlmann camp! Ginny always had a stimulating game challenge, often involving two competing sides, which included the children. The games often required an easel with a big pad of paper, marking pens, and other materials she had prepared. Everyone would be drawn into the spirit of the activity and the children relished participating with the "grown-ups." All had great fun and Ginny always had prizes, many of which she had cleverly constructed or created. The same entertainment prevailed following adult dinner parties. The games were always a stimulating and enjoyable learning experience.

Use this book of games and projects to convert your home into a fun-learning camp for your family and guests as did the Ruehlmann family. Time and space do not allow me to exalt the annual Ruehlmann Easter egg hunt, but it can't be any better at the White House!

Rupert A. Doan, Judge
Court of Appeals
Cincinnati, Ohio

Introduction

Some of the simplest treasures in life are the little, day-to-day happenings that take on special significance and create enjoyable moments and memories such as the times shared with young children. This book is a compilation of many "playtime" activities that were experienced in our household over the course of raising eight children and enjoying nineteen grandchildren. Importantly, the activities helped to create a HOME that was rich in love and learning.

It is difficult to describe the warm feelings that I experience when I hear our children singing songs or see them playing games with their own children—songs and games that I had taught them years earlier, and seemed long since to forget. The happy memories return and the heart is filled with love and fond remembrances again and again.

May you and your family enjoy the "treasures" that these activities have brought to our family. Recall, reminisce, and play some of your favorite singing and base games. Farmer in the Dell, London Bridge, Looby Loo, Here We Go 'Round the Mulberry Bush, Here We Come—Where From?, Hide and Seek, Kick the Can, Mother May I?, Run Sheep Run, and Swinging Statues have maintained popularity from one generation to another and will continue to do so.

Hopefully, this book will serve as an inspiration for the most satisfying activities of all, those that adults and children share together.

Virginia J. Ruehlmann

January

New Year's Day

Centuries ago, January 1 was not recognized as New Year's Day. For many years various methods of reckoning and recording time were in existence. For example, the ancient Egyptians, Greeks, Chinese, and Romans had their own systems, some based on lunar (moon) months and some on a solar (sun) year.

Long before Christ, years were numbered from the founding of the City of Rome, which took place in 753 B.C. The practice of dating events from the birth of Christ was suggested by Dionysius in A.D. 525 but did not come into use until the ninth century A.D., about the time of Charlemagne.

Julius Caesar decided to base the calendar on the solar year, since the earth goes around the sun in just under 365-1/4 days. His intentions were to begin the New Year on December 25, the date of the winter solstice in Rome. Many people, however, liked the lunar year, and Caesar compromised by beginning his new year on the nearest new moon following December 25, 46 B.C. Later the Gregorian calendar kept this date, so our New Year's Day is on January 1.

Did you know that January was named for Janus in Roman mythology? Janus was depicted as having two faces: one looking at the months just past and the other looking forward to the year ahead.

A Snack for Birds

Make a special New Year's resolution to practice sharing with your family and friends. Start the year off right by learning the joy of giving something to God's creatures, too.

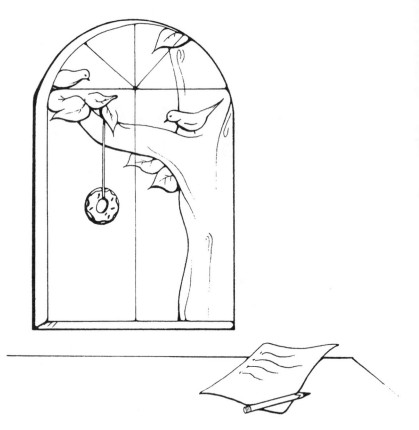

Materials Required

pinecone or stale donut
peanut butter
raisins or nuts
string or yarn

Directions

1. Spread a pinecone or stale donut with peanut butter.
2. Insert raisins or nuts into the peanut butter.
3. With a strong piece of string or yarn, tie the bird snack onto a tree near one of your windows.

4. Watch the birds eat and chirp "thank you." Keep a record of the different types of birds. Note the colorings. How many can you identify? A book or chart on local birds will help.

Playing Cards: Can You Remember?

The origin of playing cards is unknown, but many theories exist. Playing cards, professionally printed and homemade decks, have been in existence for hundreds of years in Europe and in the Orient. There is evidence that playing cards were used in France in the fourteenth century. The manufacture of playing cards in Germany dates back to the beginning of the fifteenth century, in Italy, 1425, and in England, 1463. Suits varied and included bells, hearts, leaves, swords, and money. The present-day deck with four trump suits of hearts, spades, diamonds, and clubs was adopted in France in the sixteenth century. Speculation has it that the early American Indians had their own games of chance and memory using hand-painted and dyed leather.

Memory games not only are fun but help develop the power of concentration and the ability to remember. Developing a good memory is

a skill that will benefit you throughout life and will help you with schoolwork.

Materials Required

two decks of cards

Directions

1. Select a number of matching pairs from the decks: two jacks of hearts, two threes of diamonds, two nines of hearts, two queens of spades, two aces of clubs, etc.
2. Shuffle these cards. Place facedown in equal rows—maybe four rows across and six rows down.
3. Players take turns turning over two cards at a time, trying to match a pair. If a pair is not found on a turn, the cards are put facedown again. Each time a pair is turned up, the player who successfully matches the pair removes it from the playing surface and keeps it in front of him or her.
4. Whoever matches the most pairs wins the game, because that player could remember where the pairs were.

A Crystal Garden Inside

When was the last time you saw crystals? Or ate them? Or walked on them? Or threw them? If you ever made a snowball, walked along a sandy beach, or sprinkled sugar on your cereal or salt on your french fries, then you saw, used, walked on, and ate crystals. Webster defines a crystal as "a body formed by a substance solidifying so that it has flat surfaces in a regular, even arrangement—as snow or ice crystals." Did you know that you can create a beautiful crystal garden? Try it.

Materials Required

small pieces of coal or charcoal briquettes
1/4 cup table salt
1/4 cup liquid laundry bluing

1 tablespoon household ammonia
1/4 cup water
1 glass pie plate or bowl
food coloring

Directions

1. Cover the bottom of the pie plate with the coal pieces or briquettes.
2. Combine the salt, bluing, ammonia, and water.
3. Pour the solution over the pieces of coal to soak it.
4. Squeeze a few drops of various colors of food coloring on top. Watch the beautiful crystals grow. Additional solution may be added after a few days as needed. Caution is necessary with very small children, because ammonia is a chemical compound with irritating vapors. It should be used with caution since prolonged exposure or inhalation can affect the skin, eyes, and respiratory system. It should not be tasted or consumed.

How quickly did crystals appear? How long did they last?

We Are All in the Family of God

Materials Required

a book from the library about a child of a minority group
different kinds of apples

Directions

1. Read the story.
2. Serve the apples: red skinned, yellow skinned, green skinned. All are apples and all are created by God. Just as are all people. The difference is only in the pigmentation of the skin.

How Many Days in a Month?

Thirty days have September,
April, June, and November.
All the rest have thirty-one
Except February, which has twenty-eight,
Although leap year is the time
When February has twenty-nine.

—Author Unknown

Directions

1. Have the child hold the left palm face down. With that hand make a fist.
2. Notice there are "mountains" (the knuckles) and "valleys" (the spaces between).

3. With the knuckles upright, start at the knuckle of the small finger and touch each mountain and valley with the pointer finger of the right hand while saying the names of the months. After July, start over on the same mountain and go backward.
4. Those months with 31 days are those on each mountain, and those with 30 days—or less in the case of February (28 or 29)—are in each valley.

Jigsaw Puzzles

Jigsaw puzzles were invented around 1760 by John Spilsbury, owner of a print shop at Russell Court in Covent Garden, England. He mounted beautifully engraved and hand-colored maps on sheets of mahogany, and with a very fine marquetry saw cut along the boundaries of the counties and countries, and created the first jigsaw puzzles. Spilsbury advertised his skill in a 1763 London street directory with the following description: "Engraver and map dissector in wood, in order to facilitate the teaching of geography." These first puzzles were very expensive and packaged in beautiful wooden boxes.

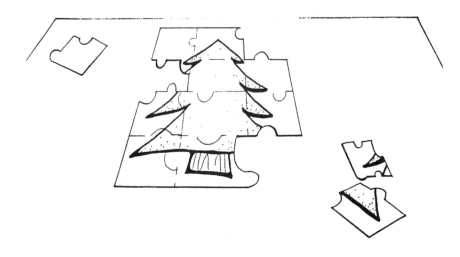

Materials Required

used greeting cards
paste
construction paper or thin cardboard
scissors

Directions

1. Use the front picture of a greeting card or Christmas card and paste it to a piece of strong construction paper or cardboard.
2. Carefully cut the card into difficult or easy shapes appropriate to the ages of the children.
3. Mix the pieces and try to assemble the jigsaw puzzle.
4. Alternative activity: Draw your own picture and proceed with steps 1, 2, and 3.

Magazine Scavenger Hunt

On a rainy day when everyone must stay indoors, plan a scavenger hunt by way of "walking through magazines."

Materials Required

similar magazines, one for each participant
lists of items to find

Directions

1. Each participant or team receives a magazine and a list of items to find.
2. Check off each item as you find it, noting the page number on which it was found.
3. The first person or team to complete the hunt wins.

Sample List

1. one boy
2. two girls
3. three fruits
4. four flowers
5. man in a suit
6. grandmother
7. telephone
8. piece of candy
9. mother and a baby
10. dog
11. tree
12. house
13. bottle of milk
14. airplane
15. boat

Warm and Rosy Apple Drink

Enjoy some warmed apple juice. The aroma from this drink permeates the entire home and adds to the feeling of warmth, security, and love.

Ingredients Required

64 oz. bottle of apple juice
3 oz. red hot cinnamon candies

1/4 cup light brown sugar
3 cinnamon sticks
several whole cloves
saucepan or crock pot
measuring cup
wooden spoon

Directions

1. Adult supervision is necessary.
2. Pour one cup of the juice into the pan.
3. Add the red cinnamon candies. Place over low heat, stirring until the candies are melted. Use a wooden spoon and stir with care. The candies have a tendency to stick together and clump but will eventually dissolve.
4. Add the rest of the juice, cinnamon sticks, brown sugar, and whole cloves. Continue to warm until time to serve. Serve in cups or mugs.

This is good any time but especially on a cold, rainy, or snowy night, at Thanksgiving time, or during the Christmas season.

Words of Magic

Some magicians use a wand and the word *Alakazaam* when they perform their magic tricks. Others repeat the words of Ali Baba and say, "Open, Sesame." You can learn two magic words of your very own and amaze everyone you meet by your politeness.

There are two little magic words
That will open any door with ease;
One little word is *thanks*
And the other little word is *please.*
—Author Unknown

Materials Required

small pieces of paper
crayons

Print Thanks on several pieces of paper. During the next week whenever anyone does an action for which they could be thanked, give them one of your slips of paper. Put a smiling face on the slips, because that's what this magic brings about: smiles.

February

Groundhog Day

According to legend, the groundhog awakens from hibernation (winter sleep) on February 2. As he emerges from his hiding place, he looks for his shadow. If he sees it, he runs back inside and sleeps for another six weeks—a signal to us that there will be six more weeks of winter. If it's cloudy out and he doesn't see his shadow, we interpret that to mean spring will break through winter early.

It seems contradictory that if the sun is shining there will be more winter, and if the sky is cloudy winter is over. But that is the legend of long standing. This idea of the groundhog predicting the weather stems from early German settlers who brought the tradition with them from their homeland, where a badger or a bear is considered the "weather prophet."

An ancient legend, origin unknown, is summed up in the following oft-repeated rhyme:

> If Candlemas Day [February 2] be fair and bright,
> winter will have another flight;
> But if it be dark with clouds and rain,
> winter is gone and won't come again.

Shadows and Silhouettes

We know where to find our shadows on a sunny day, but do you know where to find your silhouette? A silhouette is defined as a profile or outline of a person or object filled in with a solid color, usually black.

It is fun to observe a person's shadow, make a silhouette, or create interesting shadows that represent animals by using your hands and fingers.

Materials Required

sunshine or a lamp
white and black construction paper
pencils, markers, or chalk
scissors

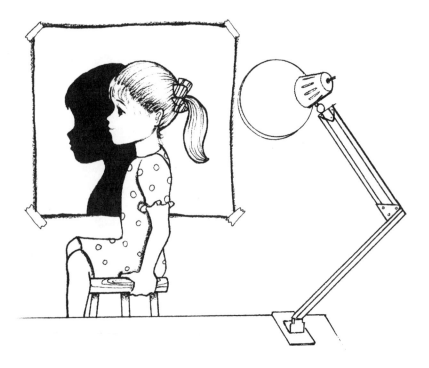

Directions

1. Adult supervision required.
2. Have the child sit sideways on a chair next to a wall.
3. Tape white construction paper on the wall next to the child's head.
4. Set up a very bright light or lamp so that the child's profile shadow is cast onto the paper, and carefully trace around the shadow.

5. Tape a sheet of black construction paper behind the white sheet. Cut out the silhouettes from both sheets at the same time.
6. Paste the black silhouette on a piece of white paper, the white silhouette on black. Add the child's name and the date.
7. Outside on a sunny day, trace the child's shadow on the cement sidewalk or driveway. Draw in some funny outfits with colored chalk.

How Tall Are You?

It's fun to observe and record the growth of a child. Try this twist on catching your child on the grow!

Materials Required

A blank plastered wall in your home, or a cement wall in
your basement
pencil
colored chalk or crayons
tape measure
sheet of paper

Directions

1. Choose an image, such as a tree or giraffe, as a means of recording and comparing the height of the child and/or parents.
2. Sketch an outline of that image on your sheet of paper, or use a
   picture from a book as a guide. Do an enlarged version in chalk
   on the designated wall space. When you are satisfied with the
   looks of it, add some colors. If you cannot draw directly on the
   wall, use poster board and tape it to the wall.
3. Measure your child or children. If you chose a tree for your picture, a branch or a freshly drawn apple can be the indicator. Be
   sure to include the name, measurement, date, and year.

Decorated Valentine Box

Materials Required

empty box (shoe-box size is fine)
red construction paper
paste
doilies
scraps of ribbon, lace
scissors

Directions

1. Paste paper doilies around the box and on the top of the lid.
2. Fold a piece of red construction paper in half and cut out a heart as shown. Repeat.
3. Paste the hearts on the sides of the box.
4. Decorate the box with bows, ribbon, or lace.
5. Cut an opening in the top of the lid so that valentines can be inserted.
6. Using step 2, make some valentines to give to your family and friends.
7. Part of the fun of any celebration includes planning or preparing a snack. Buy or bake heart-shaped cookies and serve with a glass of red punch.

Ruby Red Fruit Punch

1 46-oz. can red fruit punch
1 liter bottle either lemon-lime soda or creme soda
1 pint lemon sherbet

1 frozen ice ring or heart-shaped mold made the day before. Be original. Add thin slices of lemon or maraschino cherries or strawberries. Pour fruit punch into serving bowl. Add the sherbet. Pour the soda over the sherbet. Slip the ice ring into the bowl. Makes approximately 16 6-oz. servings.

Hearts in the Hat

Materials Required

heart cards from decks of playing cards
a man's hat or a small basket

Directions

1. Place the hat or basket next to the wall and mark off a line several feet away.
2. Take turns throwing five cards, one at a time, toward the hat. The object is to have the card land in the hat.
3. Keep score. A card that lands in the hat scores two points. A card that hits the wall first and then lands in the hat scores one point.
4. The person with the most points wins the title of King or Queen of Hearts.

Lincoln's and Washington's Birthdays

The birthday of each of these two famous presidents was celebrated for years on the actual birthdates: February 12 for Lincoln and February 22 for Washington.

Abraham Lincoln was born February 12, 1809, and assassinated on April 14, 1865, by John Wilkes Booth while attending a performance at the Ford Theater. Lincoln was the sixteenth president of the United States and is remembered for guiding our country through the Civil War (1861–65), The Gettysburg Address (November 19, 1863), and for his Emancipation Proclamation, which declared an end to slavery in the United States. The formal Emancipation Proclamation was issued on January 1, 1863.

George Washington, known as the father of our country, was our first president and the first man to be recognized by the United States with a holiday in his honor. Washington was born February 22, 1732, in Virginia. He was commander of the American Army during the Revolutionary War, presided over the convention of the new nation at Philadelphia, and was elected unanimously to the presidency of the new nation. After serving two terms as president and declining a third term, he retired to his home, Mount Vernon. He died December 14, 1799.

In honor of Washington and Lincoln, many states now observe one holiday called President's Day on the third Monday in February.

Washington's Tricornered Hat

In Washington's day, the most expensive hats were made of beaver fur. Whatever fabric was used, the hat had to be rigid enough to be shaped into a tricornered, or three-horned, hat patterned after the formal hats worn in Europe at that time. Triangular in shape, the hat had three cocked flaps of equal size. It was worn uncocked only in bad weather or by rebellious youths of the day. The trim, usually of braid, feathers, or lace, often indicated one's profession and rank. Washington undoubtedly wore this style hat also.

Materials Required

12″–14″ round tray
1 large brown grocery sack or thin cardboard
markers or crayons
scissors
red, white, blue scraps of ribbon
tape measure

Directions

1. Split the ends and one side of the brown sack.
2. Place tray in center and trace around it with a blue crayon. Cut out this circle.
3. Measure child's head and cut out an appropriate area from the center of your brown circle (approximately a five-inch circle). It should be large enough to fit on top of the head.

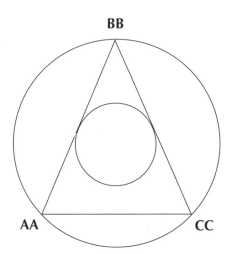

4. Imagine a triangle surrounding the hole for the head. Fold along the three lines of the triangle, making three brims. Color them blue on both sides. Paste the red, white, and blue ribbon on the front brim for decoration. Staple or tape folded-up corners together: A to A, B to B, C to C, for stability.
5. Make hats for your friends and plan a parade.

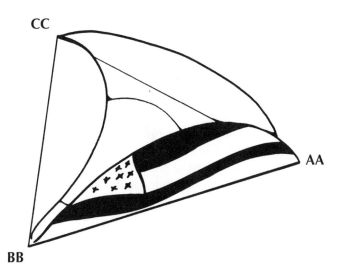

Presidents on Coins and Bills

Lincoln and Washington are the presidents whose pictures are best known and easily identified on coins and bills.

Materials Required

penny
quarter
one-dollar bill
five-dollar bill
magnifying glass

Review stories about Lincoln and Washington. Have their pictures available. As the youngster looks through the magnifying glass, ask interesting questions, such as, "Who is on the penny? Why, do you think, was Lincoln's image used on the penny? Does he look the same as on the five-dollar bill? What extra details can you observe on the bill that you couldn't see on the penny?" Talk about the manner in which Washington is wearing his hair on the quarter (a formal wig).

Try placing coins between two sheets of plain notebook paper and rub over with crayon. You have created a "rubbing."

February Salad and Dessert

Plan a complete menu that you can make together—if not the entire meal, at least dessert or salad.

Indgredients and Materials Required

Salad

1 3-oz. box cherry gelatin
1 can Queen Anne cherries
individual dessert dishes or one large bowl
prepare as for a fruit-gelatin salad
or

Dessert

ready-made graham cracker crust or shaped toast points
1 can cherry pie filling
1 package instant pudding or pie filling
2 cups milk
cupcake tin

Directions

1. Decide on making either cherry salad or cherry dessert.
2. Make a centerpiece of rolled brown construction paper for a log and a paper ax handle. Use foil for the make-believe blade.
3. Tell or have read the story about Washington and the cherry tree, Lincoln and the log cabin. Explain that the cherry tree story is only a legend.
4. Impress the children with the value of honesty.
5. Adult supervision is required. Heat oven to 375 degrees. While it's heating, make the toast shells. Remove crusts from a thin slice of bread. Spread each slice with softened margarine or butter, sprinkle with a mixture of sugar and cinnamon. Press a prepared slice into each cupcake tin. When oven is heated, turn off. Place cupcake tin with bread into the turned-off oven for 15 minutes.
6. While the toast shells are in the oven, mix the instant pudding and milk according to the directions on the package. Spoon some pudding into each toast shell or into the ready-made graham cracker pie shell. Spoon some cherry pie filling on top of the pudding. Refrigerate until time to eat and enjoy.

Compliments

Isn't it nice to receive a compliment or hear an unexpected word of praise or love? Surprise someone with a kind remark, and you will be surprised yourself at how good it makes you feel.

Materials Required

paper
crayons
pencil

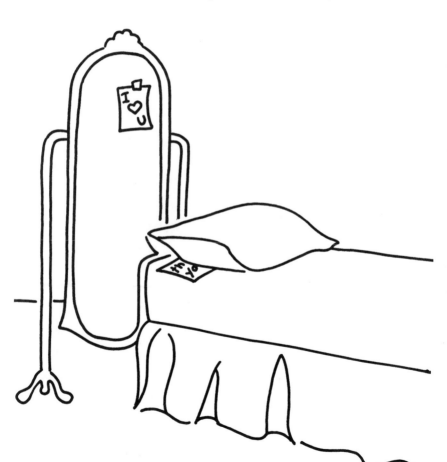

Directions

1. Draw a heart or some object that you like. Print "I love you" or "Thank you for ———."
2. Place it under mother's, dad's, sister's, brother's, grandmother's, or grandfather's pillow for the recipient to find later as a surprise.
3. You may want to tape the message to a mirror or put it under the person's plate to be discovered at mealtime.

March

Two Little Birds

For the young child and for the young at heart this is a good month to learn more about birds. Learning can be done in the house and outside.

Materials Required

blue paper
tape
dexterity in your fingers
song in your voice

Directions

1. Use two strips of tape colored blue or blue paper.
2. Wrap each strip around the right and left index fingers.
3. Close your other fingers together and place underneath your palms as you extend your two index fingers and say the following:

> Two little blue birds sitting on a hill;
> One named Jack and one named Jill.

"Fly away, Jack" (raise your right finger as high as your right ear) "and fly away, Jill" (raise your left finger as high as your left ear). As you recite the remaining lines, fold back your index finger and extend middle finger before bringing your hand down and into view. It appears as if the bird has disappeared. In truth, it is just folded under your palm waiting for you to reverse the procedure and bring the birds back when you finish the verse, saying, "Come back, Jack, come back, Jill."

4. Practice makes perfect. Little ones adore this.
5. Take a walk around your yard, neighborhood, or a park. Watch for signs of birds returning to your area. How many of the birds in your neighborhood can you identify? Did you see any bird nests?

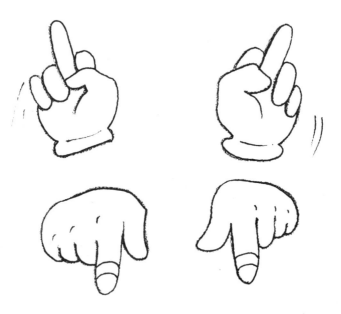

Chunky Chalk
for Young Sidewalk Artists

Enjoy drawing artwork, designs, hopscotch squares, or printing on the sidewalk with chunky chalk.

Materials Required

plaster of paris
small paper cups
water
measuring spoon
spoon for stirring

Directions

1. Measure four tablespoons of the dry plaster into each cup—one cup for each child.
2. Completing one cup at a time, add four tablespoons of water to each cup and stir immediately until smooth and the thickness of sour cream.
3. Remove the spoon and place it in water to prevent any plaster from hardening.
4. The plaster-and-water solution will become warm to the touch.
5. Let the mixture harden for at least two to three days.
6. Tear off the paper cup.
7. Your chalk should be ready to use. Happy drawing.

Four Seasons of the Year

Materials Required

four sheets of paper
crayons

winter

spring

summer

fall

Directions

If you have an apple tree in your own yard, have the child observe it. If not, take a walk around the neighborhood or go to a local park. Call attention to the beautiful white blossoms.

Have the child draw his or her perception of the apple tree. Hang this picture at home or save in a file. Repeat this procedure for all four seasons—spring, summer, fall, and winter. Note the differences. Hang the four pictures together. Have the artist sign each one.

Nutshell Animals

Materials Required

walnut-shell halves
white paint
pink beads or pink sequins or pink felt
tiny black beads or black felt
white thread
cotton balls
gray, green, white construction paper
glue
pink crayon
scissors
yarn, string, or rubber band
marbles

Directions

1. To make a rabbit, first paint the shells white. Set aside to dry completely.
2. Using a toothpick, apply glue to the pink beads and place onto the shell. If you have opted for the pink felt, try a paper punch to get the small circles to glue on for the eyes.

3. The whiskers are made by folding a 6" piece of coarse white thread into six strands, each about 1" in length. Tie securely in the center. Knot several times.

4. Cut teeth and ears from the white paper according to the pattern. Color the inside of the ears pink. Glue the ears and teeth in place.

5. For the finishing touch, glue on a small piece of cotton to represent the tail.

6. You can also make adorable mice from walnut shells. Leave shells the natural color or paint them gray. Use gray construction paper or felt for the little rounded ears. Add a touch of pink to the insides of the ears. Glue some tiny black beads or small black felt circles for the eyes. Make the whiskers the same way but use black thread. For the tail, use a piece of gray yarn or a section of a rubber band.

7. You can also make a terrific turtle from a walnut shell. Cut a piece of green construction paper enlarging the pattern below. Create designs on the shell with markers. Use the cut-out pattern to make the base for the turtle. Glue the shell onto the base.

8. To make a racing game, place a marble under each nutshell friend. Make a ramp from a cookie sheet or tray. One, two, three, release! Watch your friends race down the ramp. Care must be taken so that young children do not put the marbles in their mouths.

mouse pattern

fold & glue
TEETH

fold & glue
EARS

Turtle pattern

Individual Pizzas

Long before pizza parlors baked and delivered pizza on order, fun and tasty treats were made by helping hands in the home kitchen.

Ingredients and Materials Required

1 package sandwich-size buns
1 can tomato soup undiluted
1 can cream of mushroom soup undiluted
1 teaspoon oregano
dash tabasco sauce
1/2 teaspoon sugar
1 package shredded mozzarella cheese
grated Parmesan cheese
toppings of your choice: mushrooms, pepperoni, etc.
cookie sheet
mixing bowl
large spoon

Directions

1. Adult supervision is needed.
2. Preheat oven to 375 degrees.
3. Slice the buns in half.

4. Place the open halves onto the cookie sheet, making sure that the cut surfaces are facing up and the crusty sides down. Place in the oven for 10 minutes.
5. While the bun halves are getting a little toasted, mix the soups, oregano, sugar, and tabasco sauce together in a mixing bowl.
6. Remove the buns from the oven. Spoon the soup mixture onto the top of each bun half. Sprinkle the cheese on top. Add any extra toppings that you desire.
7. Return to oven for 15 minutes or until bubbly.
8. Make enough to have a pizza party.

Kites

Although air, a mixture of gases, is invisible, it affects other objects. Observe this while having fun flying a kite outside or gliding a paper airplane. inside the house.

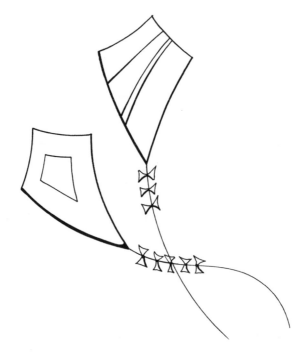

It is quite possible to make your own kites by using materials available around the house, such as brown paper, tissue paper or plastic sacks, dowel sticks or thin sticks from trees, glue, tape, string, ribbon, and small pieces of fabric.

For the beginner, purchase an inexpensive kite kit at the store. Assemble according to package instructions. Have plenty of string available, if possible, a kite-winder. Be sure to add a tail to the kite.

When the weather clears and the wind is blowing quite briskly, plan a family kite-flying party. What causes the kite to stay up? Whose kite went the highest? Whose stayed up the longest?

Quick-as-a-Bunny Cupcakes

Materials Required

yellow, white, or lemon cake mix
white icing
white construction paper

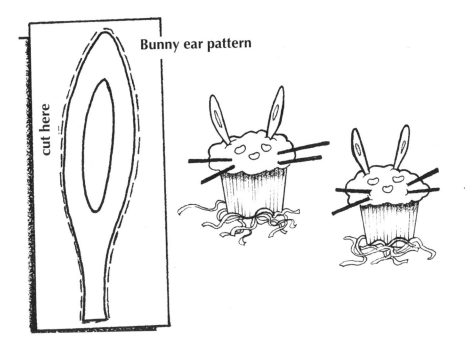

Bunny ear pattern

cut here

pink crayon
tiny jelly beans or miniature bird-egg candies
black string licorice candy

Directions

1. Prepare the cupcakes according to the instructions on the box. Cool and spread with white icing.
2. Cut enough construction paper ears, allowing two to a cupcake, according to the pattern. Color the inside of the ears pink and place on the cupcakes.
3. Place a red candy for the mouth and two pink ones for the eyes. Cut the licorice into pieces to use for whiskers.

Saint Patrick's Day

Saint Patrick's Day is celebrated on March 17 all over the world wherever the Irish gather. Most authorities agree that St. Patrick was

born in southwestern England around A.D. 373. When he was sixteen years of age, some Irish raiders kidnapped him and took him as a slave to Ireland. There he tended the sheep of an Irish chieftain for six years until he managed to escape aboard a ship bound for France. He lived in France for many years and eventually became a bishop.

Directed by a vision, he returned to Ireland as a missionary in 432 and worked diligently to establish Christianity there. Using the three-leafed shamrock as a visual aid, he explained that the Holy Trinity consists of three Persons, all equal, yet one Person. Through the years, the shamrock has continued to hold a place of special significance among the Irish people.

Leprechaun Magic

March 17 is St. Patrick's Day and a good day to see some green magic.

Materials Required

a white carnation or an inner stalk of celery with leaves
a clear glass
water
absorbent paper towel
cotton ball
sponge
green food coloring

Directions

1. Explain about leprechauns and their mischievous ways, their pots of gold, and their love for the color green. A library book may help.
2. Fill the clear glass with water and add several drops of green food coloring.

3. Using the knife and with adult help make a 1" slit in the end of the carnation or the stalk of celery and place in the glass of green water. The flower or celery leaves should remain above the water level.

4. After 30 minutes observe the flower petals or the celery. Observe again in two hours. Wait until the next day and observe the colorings. Explain to the child that absorption has occurred—or maybe the leprechauns have done it again!

Paper Cup Telephone

Alexander Graham Bell was the inventor of the telephone. On March 10, 1876, Bell spoke the first sentence to be transmitted through electric waves when he said to his assistant, "Watson, come here. I want you." You can make a paper cup telephone of your own.

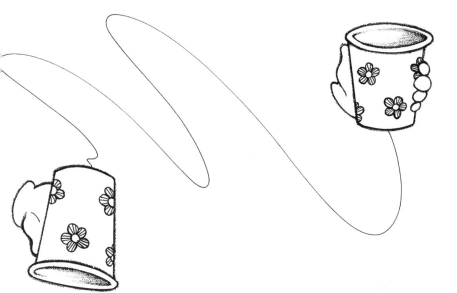

Materials Required

2 empty 10 oz. paper cups
10-foot length of twine
masking tape
nail or darning needle

Directions

1. With the nail or darning needle, create a small hole in the bottom of each cup.
2. Carefully thread the string through the bottom end of each cup and into the hole. Tie knots in the ends of the string to prevent it from slipping out of the cups.
3. Stretch the string full length. It must be taut. The caller talks into the open end of one of the cups, while the listener places the open end of the other cup close to his or her ear. Explain that the vibrations travel along the string and into the cup. As the listener's ear feels the vibrations, he or she hears the words.
4. This is a good time to teach the child the home telephone number and 911.

April

Do you recall this rhyme from years ago?

April one day was asked whether
She could give reliable weather.
She laughed 'til she cried
And said, "Bless you, I've tried,
But I do get things mixed up together."
—Author Unknown

April Fools' Day

The first of April has long been called April Fools' Day and is devoted to playing harmless jokes. It is believed that the custom of "April fooling" began in Europe when New Year's Day was changed on the calendar. In olden days, New Year's Day was celebrated on March 25, accompanied with feasting until April 1. In 1564, France changed the date of the New Year to January 1, with confusion resulting. Some people clung to the old calendar, and to ridicule them, jokes and false errands were perpetrated throughout the day on April 1.

Airplanes

So you have a rainy day? Make some paper airplanes and glide them in the house. Whose plane glides farthest? Award a "Longest Flight" or "Best Pilot" medal.

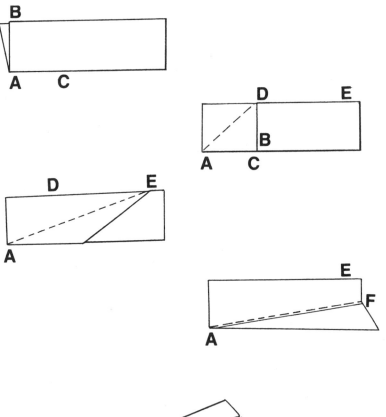

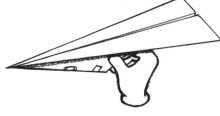

Materials Required

8-1/2″-by-11″ piece of construction paper or newspaper
tape
crayon or marker to identify plane
paper clip

Directions

1. Fold paper in half lengthwise. Crease the fold.
2. Fold the corners at one end down and outward, creating the triangle nose of the plane. Crease folds.
3. Repeat the folding procedure two more times, each time creasing the fold. Your paper will now look like a long, thin triangle.
4. Allow the top flaps to extend, and tape the inner flaps together.
5. Decorate with numbers and initials. Ready for takeoff! Try putting a paper clip on the bottom and see what happens.

Butterflies

What is more suggestive of springtime than the sight of a beautiful butterfly? Add a touch of happiness with butterflies of your own making.

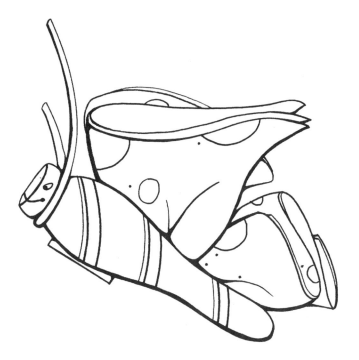

Materials Required

clothespins (old-fashioned type, not clip)
2 paper napkins, each 6″ square, left folded
or appropriately sized colored tissue paper
markers or crayons
scissors
scraps of ricrac and sequins
magnet strip
pipe cleaner
glue

Directions

1. For the large wings, fold one folded paper napkin in half, thus having 8 thicknesses. Fold the other folded napkin into thirds, thus having a smaller but thicker set of wings. Create designs with markers or crayons. You may prefer to glue on bits of ricrac and sequins.
2. With a marker or crayon color the clothespin as the head and body of the butterfly.
3. Glue the magnet onto the underside of the clothespin. Spread a little glue between the prongs as well.
4. Gather and slide the larger wings between the prongs of the clothespin. Now gather and slide the smaller set into place.
5. Twist the pipe cleaner around the neck of the clothespin and extend the ends forward. Your butterfly is ready to fly onto the refrigerator.

Easter

Although Easter is the celebration of the resurrection of Jesus, the word *Easter* is derived from the ancient Anglo-Saxon goddess of spring named Easter. A festival of spring was always held in her honor in the month of April. It is from this old pagan festival that many of our modern Easter customs originate.

Easter always comes on a Sunday in commemoration of Jesus' resurrection. The date, however, fluctuates. Easter is always the first Sunday that follows the Paschal full moon, which appears after the vernal equinox.

Easter Eggs

Many people in ancient civilizations regarded the egg as an emblem of life—a new beginning. Christians borrowed the egg for use in their Easter celebrations and festivities but used it as a symbol of the resurrection, comparing the egg to a tomb from which new life emerges.

Directions

Add interesting designs to your colored eggs. After the eggs are hard boiled, but before they are colored, place different widths of rubber bands around the eggs in various directions. Leave the bands on the hard-boiled eggs when you dip them to be colored. Pretty designs are automatically created on each egg, for the color will not penetrate the rubber, leaving white stripes.

Arbor Day

April 22, 1872, was originally proclaimed Arbor Day by the state of Nebraska through the efforts of J. Sterling Morton, who recognized the need and value of planting trees in his state. More than a million trees were planted at that time in Nebraska, where treeless plains abounded. Arbor is derived from the Latin word for tree. Through the years, planting trees on Arbor Day has spread from Nebraska to most of the United States and Canada. Arbor Day varies from state to state. In most of the northern states, Arbor Day is celebrated in April or May. In the southern states, Arbor Day occurs sometime between December and March. In Ohio, the last Friday in April is recognized as Arbor Day, but Kentucky designates the first Friday of April as its Arbor Day. The important fact is that the planting of trees continues

throughout our country and accomplishes much good for our environment and also enhances a community's beauty.

"Johnny Appleseed," whose real name was John Chapman, did much to encourage the planting and growth of apple trees. Although he was born in Springfield, Massachusetts, in 1775, he is best known for his planting of appleseeds—and trees—in Ohio around 1801. Wouldn't it be fun to read a book about "Johnny Appleseed"?

Seeds Take Root

Materials Required

small clay flowerpot
or small plastic cup
potting soil
grapefruit or orange seeds
or a few beans

Directions

1. If using the plastic cup, poke a tiny drain hole in the bottom. The clay pot should already have one. Add some soil.
2. Soak the seeds for an hour. Plant them in the dirt.
3. Place the cup or pot on a saucer or plastic lid and set it on the windowsill. Watch what happens in the next several days. (Keep the soil moist but not wet.)

Hopscotch

Hopscotch is a game youngsters love. It involves the skill of tossing a flat stone, puck, or iron washer into a designated area and the ability to hop. For very young children a variation should be used until the dexterity of balance is perfected and the expertise of hopping is well developed.

A court similar to the diagram included here is drawn on the sidewalk with chalk, or a permanent one can be painted.

Home rules apply in friendly backyard games, but strict rules and violations are followed in true tournaments. For home play, rules can permit variations that include resting in spaces 2 and 3, landing on both feet in spaces 5 and 6, and 8 and 9. Arc 10 requires special home rules as well.

When a player misses, the next player begins and tries to get farther in play before a miss.

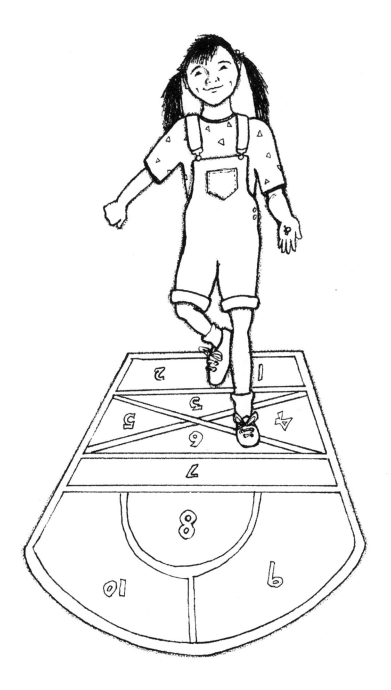

Rules

1. Throw puck into square number 1. Hop into square number 1 and without touching any lines, pick up puck and return to starting line.
2. Continue by throwing puck into square number 2. Hop into number 1 and number 2, then pick puck out of square number 2 as per rule one. Hop into square number 1 on return to base line.
3. Throw puck into triangle number 3. Jump into number 1 and number 2 at the same time. Hop into number 3 and pick puck out of triangle number 3. Then jump into number 1 and number 2 at the same time on the return trip.
4. Throw puck into triangle number 4. Jump into number 1 and number 2 at the same time. Hop into number 3, hop into number 4, and pick up puck out of triangle number 4. Then hop into triangle number 3 and jump into numbers 2 and 1 at the same time on the return trip.
5. Throw puck into triangle number 5. Jump into number 1 and number 2 at the same time. Hop into number 3, hop into number 4, hop into number 5, and pick puck out of triangle number 5. Then hop into number 4, hop into number 3, and jump into number 2 and number 1 at the same time on the return trip.
6. Throw puck into triangle number 6. Jump into number 1 and number 2 at the same time. Hop into triangle number 3, jump with both feet into triangle number 4 and number 5, hop into number 6 and pick puck out of number 6. Then jump into number 5 and number 4 at the same time, hop into number 3, and jump into number 2 and number 1 at the same time on the return trip.
7. Throw puck into rectangle number 7. Jump into number 1 and number 2 at the same time. Hop into number 3. Jump into number 4 and number 5, hop into number 6, jump with both feet into number 7, pick puck out of number 7. Hop into number 6, jump into number 5 and number 4, hop into number 3, jump into number 2 and number 1 at the same time on the return trip.
8. Throw puck into semicircle number 8. Jump into number 1 and number 2, hop into number 3, jump into number 4 and number 5, hop into number 6, jump into number 7, jump into number 8, pick up puck. Jump into number 7, hop into number 6, jump

into number 5 and number 4, hop into number 3. Jump into number 2 and number 1 on the return trip.

9. Throw puck into quarter arc number 9. Jump into 1 and 2. Hop into 3, jump into 4 and 5, hop into 6. Jump into 7, jump into 8, hop into 9, and pick up the puck. Jump into 8, jump into 7, hop into 6, jump into 5 and 4, hop into 3, jump into 2 and 1 on the return trip.

10. Throw puck into quarter arc number 10. Jump into 1 and 2, hop into 3, jump into 4 and 5, hop into 6. Jump into 7, jump into 8, hop into 9, reach into 10 and pick up the puck. Jump into 8, jump into 7, hop into 6, jump into 5 and 4, hop into 3, jump into 2 and 1 on the return trip.

11. Without puck jump into 1 and 2, hop into 3, jump into 4 and 5, hop into 6, jump into 7, jump into 8, jump into 9 and 10 at the same time. Jump into 10 and 9 at the same time, jump into 8, jump into 7, hop into 6, jump into 5 and 4, hop into 3, jump into 2 and 1 on the return trip.

Violations

1. Puck may not rest on a line or lines.
2. Jumps and hops may not touch line or lines.
3. If a player violates a rule, the turn is lost; but the next time the player comes back, player begins where he or she left off. (For example, triangle number 6 is missed first turn. Begin next turn by throwing puck into number 6.)

O'Leary

Another popular activity that has sustained the test of time is the game of O'Leary, played as an individual bounces a small rubber ball while performing a routine or specific actions.

Neighborhood play can vary in many ways and sequences from the tournament required movements. Actions also vary according to sources and geographic locations.

During the performance of the stunts in O'Leary, the following rhyme is sung:

1-2-3 O'Leary, 4-5-6 O'Leary, 7-8-9 O'Leary, 10 O'Leary postman.

Bat the ball with the flat of the hand to 1-2-3 and do the prescribed movement each time to the word O'Leary; to O'Leary postman give one bounce to "10." Do prescribed movement to the word O'Leary, bat the ball with the flat of the hand at the word "post" and catch on "man." The ball is never caught until the last.

Exercise 1
Swing right leg outward over ball on saying O'Leary.

Exercise 2
Swing left leg inward over ball on saying O'Leary.

Exercise 3
Swing right leg outward over ball saying O'Leary, clapping hands together at each bounce and under leg at O'Leary.

Exercise 4
Swing left leg inward over ball on saying O'Leary, clapping hands together at each bounce and under leg at O'Leary.

Exercise 5
Grasp right wrist with left hand forming circle with arms and make the ball pass through from below upon saying O'Leary.

Exercise 6
Same as exercise 5, letting ball drop over from above.

Exercise 7
Grasp edge of shorts (or long pants just above the knee) with left hand and upon saying O'Leary make the ball pass upward between the arm and shorts, batting the ball on regular rhythm.

Exercise 8
Same as exercise 7, but let ball pass through downward from above.

Exercise 9
Same as exercise 7, but use right hand and let ball pass through downward from above.

Exercise 10
Heel, toe, heel swing right leg over outward, hopping on opposite foot and heel-O'Leary-toe, heel.

Exercise 11
Heel, toe, swing left leg over, inward, hopping on opposite foot.

Exercise 12
Same as number 1, but jump over ball with both legs.

Rules

1. One hand only shall be used in bouncing the ball.
2. Ball shall be bounced only once, no double bounce allowed.
3. If ball is caught in any other way than called for by the exercise, it shall constitute a "miss." The ball must be caught with one hand.
4. Any player departing from the set order of exercises shall forfeit one turn.
5. Counting shall be done in a steady, even manner so that the other players can hear it.

6. If ball is interfered with by any person other than the player in possession of the ball, player is entitled to another trial.
7. The player engaged in performing the exercise shall count.
8. If the ball hits or touches any part of the body causing the ball to be bounced, it shall count as a "miss."
9. The ball must be caught and held at the end of each exercise before the next exercise is begun.
10. In exercises in which the hand holds the shorts, the hand must be on the shorts when the ball passes through.
11. No one shall attempt to make a player miss by act or word.
12. The player's opponent shall be judge of any misplay or omission of an exercise or any part.
13. Any wrong execution of an exercise constitutes a "miss."
14. The words "1-2-3 O'Leary" must be said loud enough so that they are audible to all players.
15. The player going farthest in the O'Leary exercise without a "miss" wins.

Nature Thaumatrope

A thaumatrope is an optical toy, which when rotated quickly causes two pictures to appear as one.

Materials Required

two 7" flat, white paper plates
crayons or markers
glue or paste
tape
small wooden dowel stick,
or if unavailable use a pencil

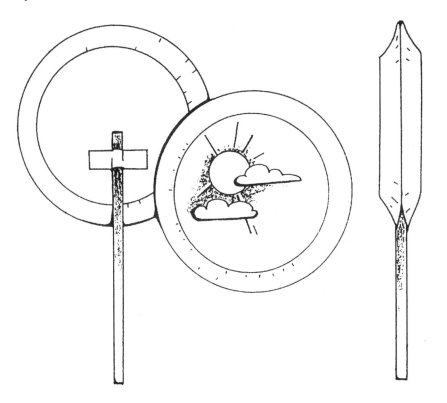

Directions

1. Decide on the scene you wish to create—a rainbow and clouds, or a chicken and eggs, or a rabbit and grass.
2. On the outside surface of one plate draw a rainbow. Put the colors in the correct order.
3. On the outside surface of the other plate draw some pretty cloud formations, blue sky, and the sun.
4. Tape the dowel stick to the inside of one of the plates, then paste or glue the two plates together. Let dry.
5. Hold the stick between both hands. Briskly and rapidly rub your hands back and forth, twirling the toy. This will make the rainbow appear in the sky picture.

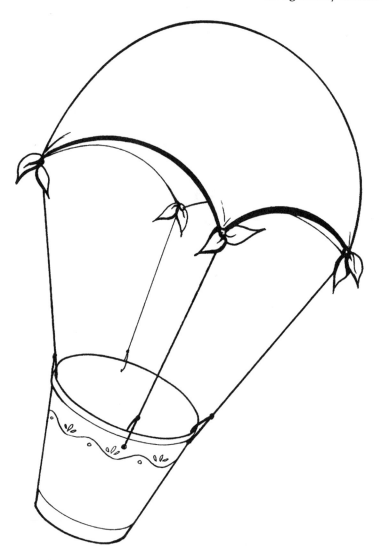

Parachutes

What do pilots always have with them when they fly? Parachutes. Make some miniature parachutes of your own.

Materials Required

man's handkerchief
or a clean cloth 10″–12″ square in size
4 equal pieces of string, each 8″ in length
a paper cup
a weight or toy figure

Directions

1. Open the handkerchief. Take the 4 equal lengths of string and tie a piece of string to each corner of the handkerchief.
2. Attach each piece of string onto a small paper cup.
3. Tape a stone, small weight, or miniature toy figure in the cup.
4. Toss into the air. Watch the parachute open and float safely to the ground.

Rainbows

April showers bring forth May flowers and often bring forth some beautiful rainbows as well. If nature doesn't provide a rainbow, make one in your own backyard.

Materials Required

a picture of a rainbow hand drawn or from a book
clear custard dishes or clear plastic cups
water
white paper
paintbrush for each child
half of white foam egg carton (with separations)
water color paints

Directions

1. On a bright sunny day place a clear glass filled two-thirds full with water on a piece of stark-white paper.
2. Gently tilt or move the glass so the sun shines through it. A rainbow will be visible on the paper.
3. When you go into the house have paper, paints, and brush available to draw rainbows and to demonstrate how blended colors are created. Show that the rainbow from the outside of its arc moving toward the inside is always red, orange, yellow, green, blue, indigo, and violet.
4. Put the colors in each egg-carton division, and let the child learn how to combine red and yellow to make orange, yellow and blue to create green, and blue and red to create purple or violet. While the color brown is not visible in the rainbow, the child can make brown by combining red, blue, and yellow.

After the summer rain, out comes the sun.
Look to the sky; what has Mother Nature done?
She has added colors—what is seen?
Red and orange, yellow and green.
Blue and purple are next in line.
Don't you agree, these colors are fine?
What has been painted; do you know—
Of course, it's a beautiful, color-filled rainbow!

Stop! Look! Listen!

Safety time is all the time.

Materials Required

construction paper: black, red, yellow, green
scissors
paste

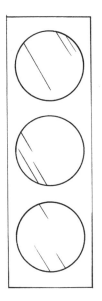

Directions

1. Use the black piece of paper as the stoplight holder.
2. Cut appropriate-sized circles from the red, yellow, and green sheets of paper.
3. Paste the red circle first, next the yellow, and next the green.
4. Teach the little ones the following rhyme:

> Stop! Look! Listen!
> Before you cross the street.
> Use your eyes, then your ears,
> And then you use your feet.

5. Repeat the rhyme each time you go for a walk.

Tasty Treat

Ingredients and Materials Required

a one-pound block of white chocolate
10-oz. shelled peanuts (preferably unsalted)
10-oz. thin pretzel sticks broken into smaller pieces
9" x 13" ovenproof pan
wooden spoon
wax paper
paper doily for decoration
cardboard box or empty cookie tin

Directions

1. Adult supervision is required.
2. Heat oven to 250 degrees.
3. Put the chocolate in the ovenproof pan and place in the warmed oven until soft.
4. Put a large piece of wax paper on a tray or cookie sheet.

5. Using oven mitts, remove pan with melted chocolate from the oven and set on a heat-resistant surface.
6. Add the peanuts and pretzel pieces and mix until all are well coated.
7. Drop by spoonfuls onto the wax paper. Form into small clusters on the wax paper. (While it is not necessary, it does help to rub the spoon with margarine before starting.)
8. When cooled completely, arrange the tasty treats in a container lined with wax paper. For gift giving or extra decoration, put a doily down first. You can make your own doily if you follow the steps of making a snowflake (see page 210–211). Adjust your paper size according to your box size.

Jumping Rope

Boys and girls should all participate. Children love to learn the rhymes to which you jumped as a child.

Teddy Bear, Teddy Bear, turn around,
Teddy Bear, Teddy Bear, touch the ground.
Teddy Bear, Teddy Bear, read the news,
Teddy Bear, Teddy Bear, show your shoes.
Teddy Bear, Teddy Bear, climb the stairs,
Teddy Bear, Teddy Bear, say your prayers.
Teddy Bear, Teddy Bear, turn out the light,
Teddy Bear, Teddy Bear, now good night.

Adults, can you remember during school recess or after dinner on warm evenings running outside to jump rope? Can you recall the words to "Down in the Valley, Where the Green Grass Grows" or "High Water, Low Water"? What else comes to mind?

Share your memories with the children.

You might choose to be "steady ender."

May

May Day
May Basket
Bird Day
Bird Nests from Brown Bags
"Bird Nest" Yummies
Bumblebee Hand Puppet
Mother's Day
Paper Flowers from Egg Cartons
Paper Flowers from Cupcake Liners
Memorial Day
Colorful Paper Hat Parade

May Day

How did the practice of making, delivering, and surprising people with May baskets ever get started? Some historians say the practice dates back to the ancient Druids who celebrated May 1 with songs and dances. Others contend that the celebration of May Day stems from Roman times when a festival in honor of Flora, the Roman goddess of flowers and springtime was observed.

In olden days in England the May Day festival always included a dance around the maypole, a pole set up on the village green decorated with flowers and long ribbons attached to the top. Groups of dancers, each dancer holding a streamer of ribbon, danced around the pole and attempted to weave their ribbons in pleasing designs. The group whose maypole design was intricately and perfectly patterned won great applause and recognition from the spectators.

Many of these customs are still carried on today. The reason for celebrating May Day developed from the natural delight of the people tired of the dreary winter weather and overjoyed at the arrival of spring with its warmth and flowers.

May Basket

Surprise someone with a May basket. Whether it is filled with paper flowers or real flowers, someone—grandmother, a parent, an aunt, a neighbor—will appreciate your thoughtfulness.

Materials Required

inexpensive white paper plate
crayons or markers
ribbon, 10″–12″ long
ricrac or lace
a few colored paper napkins
(about 12″ square when opened,
6″ square when folded in fourths)
or facial tissues
green pipe-cleaner stems
tape
green construction paper
scissors, and pinking shears if available
stapler

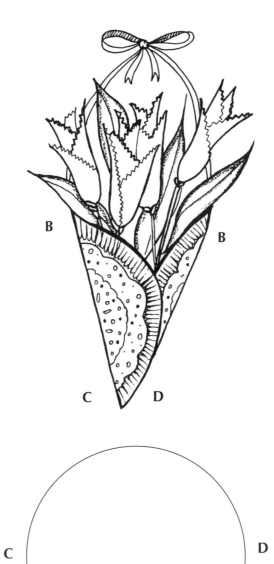

Directions

1. Decorate the bottom side of the paper plate with your own design made with markers or bits of lace and ricrac.
2. Fold plate in half without creasing through. Now holding plate at point B with one hand, fold points C and D in until they overlap. Tape or staple. Fold the ribbon in half and staple it, creating a handle for your basket.
3. Open a napkin or facial tissue. Fold it in half lengthwise. Pink both sides lengthwise. If you do not have pinking shears merely cut several V-shaped snips up and down the edges.
4. Hold the tissue or napkin in the center bottom and gather together. Twist a pipe cleaner around the center to hold in place. Open the petals. Cut some green leaves from the construction paper and tape onto the stem. Do several of different colors. Place into your May basket. A drop of cologne will add fragrance.

Bird Day

In May 1894, in Oil City, Pennsylvania, a school superintendent named C. A. Babcock originated the idea of Bird Day and initiated the observance of it in the public schools of that city. Mr. Babcock wanted the students to recognize the importance of the good done by the birds and the need to protect them.

So impressed was the United States Department of Agriculture with the idea that two years later, in 1896, a notice was issued to all public schools urging the establishment of Bird Protection Day. The actual date varies from state to state. Some schools prefer to celebrate Arbor Day and Bird Day at the same time. In Louisiana, May 5, birthday of John James Audubon, was set aside as the official day. This date was selected to honor the well-known and talented naturalist and illustrator of American bird life. At present, Iowa designates the first day of spring as Bird Day.

Bird Nests from Brown Bags

Depending on the size of the bags used, you can make a center-piece or individual favors for a "fly-up" ceremony or a graduation party.

Materials Required

brown paper lunch bags
small pieces of fabric, ribbon, string, yarn
bits of cotton
twigs

Directions

1. Open as many lunch bags as the number of nests that you wish to make. Stand each bag upright.
2. Beginning at the top of each lunch bag, roll the edges down and outward. Continue until the bag is the size and height of a bird nest.

3. Crumple and pinch the nest.
4. Place the cotton, fabric, yarn, string, and twigs in the nest.
5. Candy eggs and a feather (or a small bird from the craft store) add a nice touch.

"Bird Nest" Yummies

Take a walk around your yard, neighborhood, or a park. Watch for signs of birds returning to your area. How many of the birds in your neighborhood can you identify? Can you see any bird nests? Before your observation walk, visit the library and examine a book on birds.

Where do birds go when they fly in the sky? Why do you see many birds at different seasons of the year? What kinds of birds do you see in your neighborhood? See if you can find the answer in your books from the library. Then make the following treats.

Ingredients and Materials Required

1 12-oz. package chocolate bits
1 6-oz. package butterscotch bits
1 5-1/2-oz. can chow mein noodles
1 cup chopped nutmeats—pecans or peanuts
double boiler or microwave bowl
spoon
wax paper

Directions

1. Adult assistance is required.
2. Melt the bits in double boiler or microwave. When bits are melted, remove pan from heat and place on heat-resistant surface.
3. Add the noodles and the nuts.
4. Mix well and drop by spoonfuls onto the sheet of wax paper.

5. Before the treats harden, use the spoon to indent centers so that each treat looks like a bird nest.
6. If you desire, you may place a jelly bean or small colored candy egg in each nest.
7. Talk about the eggs of birds: size, shape, and color. Often it is possible to see birds building or occupying nests. Sometimes the birds have flown away and the nest is no longer being used. Keep your eyes open to observe, but don't disturb the home if the birds are still living there.

Bumblebee Hand Puppet

While bees may sting if we get too close to them, they are actually our friends. Bees help pollinate flowers in the garden and they make the honey that you spread on your biscuits and toast.

Buzz, buzz, buzz
Goes the busy bee;
The bee is making honey
For you and for me.

You can make a wonderful bee hand puppet using a bag and construction paper.

Materials Required

brown bag
(the size used to pack a lunch)
black, tan, and yellow construction paper
scissors
paste

Directions

1. Cut out ovals from two sheets of yellow construction paper. The ovals should be sized to fit on the bag. Paste one on top and one on the bottom of the oval.
2. Cut black strips from the black paper to paste across the yellow oval pasted on top of the bag.
3. Add two thick black strips to the head area as antennae.
4. Cut two wings from the tan construction paper. Paste one on each side of the body of the bee.
5. Slip your hand into the bag and have the bumblebee do the following actions after you memorize the rhyme:

> Bumblebee, bumblebee, you rest on my nose.
> Bumblebee, bumblebee, you sit on my toes.
> You light on my head, my ear, and my elbow,
> Then you see a flower and away you go!
>
> —Author Unknown

Mother's Day

Mother's Day is celebrated on the second Sunday in May thanks to the efforts of Ann Jarvis, who initiated the idea in honor of her own mother and held the second Mother's Day on the second Sunday in May 1908. Yes, the second Mother's Day.

The very first Mother's Day was organized by Miss Jarvis's mother in a little West Virginia town after the Civil War. She had observed the residual hard feelings between the returning soldiers, some of whom had fought for the North and some for the South. She organized a picnic for the mothers of the returned soldiers and their sons. At the conclusion of the picnic handshakes and smiles of friendship prevailed.

Six years after Miss Jarvis's successful memorial celebration in honor of her mother's efforts and in recognition of all mothers, President Woodrow Wilson issued a proclamation requesting government officials to display flags on Mother's Day, May 9, 1914. Since then the observance of Mother's Day has continued to grow and has spread to many countries.

Paper Flowers from Egg Cartons

Any month is a good month to make paper flowers, especially if you don't have real ones.

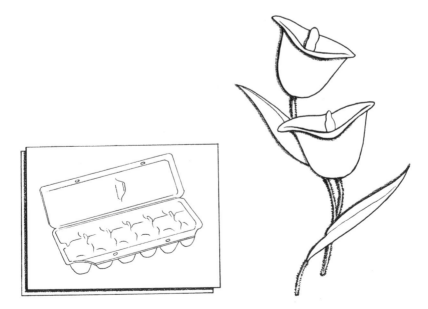

Materials Required

empty cardboard egg carton
scissors
water colors
green construction paper
pipe cleaners
small piece of cotton
nail
tape
paste

Directions

1. Cut out and separate each egg cup. Paint each one a different color. With the nail create a small hole in the bottom of each egg cup.
2. Stick a pipe cleaner through the hole and wrap and paste a small bit of cotton on the end inside of the cup. Paint it yellow.
3. Cut tulip leaves from the green construction paper and tape onto the pipe cleaner stem for each flower.

Viola! Homemade flowers!

Paper Flowers from Cupcake Liners

Another quick and enjoyable way of making paper flowers is to use cupcake liners.

Materials Required

4–5 cupcake liners for each flower
pipe cleaners or chenille stems
green construction paper
pencil
paste
scissors

Directions

1. Place the paper cupcake liners on top of each other. Feather them out with your fingers.
2. With the pencil poke two holes in the center of the stack of liners.
3. Insert one end of the cleaner up through the one hole and down the other hole. Twist this end of the cleaner around the longer portion and extend it down from the flower.
4. The longer extension represents the stem to which you can paste green leaves that you cut from the construction paper.
5. Make the flowers of different colors. Place in a basket that you make. A drop of cologne adds a fragrant touch.

Memorial Day

Memorial Day, also known as Decoration Day, has its origin in two early events. The townspeople of Coalsburg, Pennsylvania, believe that their town was the first place to celebrate a Decoration Day when Emma Hunter decorated her father's tomb with flowers in 1864. Colonel Hunter had fought in the Battle of Gettysburg in the Civil War. While in the cemetery, Miss Hunter met a woman whose son had been killed. The two women decided to meet the following year and decorate the graves.

The other event occurred in Columbus, Mississippi. On April 25, 1866, a local minister who had served as a chaplain in the confederate army led a group of compassionate women to Friendship Cemetery to decorate the graves of the dead of both sides. It was their wish to honor those who had fallen in the Battle of Shiloh.

John Logan, commander-in-chief of the Union Veterans Organization, The Grand Old Army, and Adjutant General N. P. Chapman, also of the same group, both called for an observance of decorating the graves of fallen soldiers.

The first Memorial Day ceremony, held at the National Cemetery in Arlington, was organized by the Grand Army in 1868. In 1887 the United States Congress made Memorial Day a holiday for federal government employees. Today Memorial Day is intended to honor each American service person who lost his or her life in any war in which the United States participated. In addition, many people decorate graves to honor their late relatives whether or not they served in the armed forces.

Colorful Paper Hat Parade

Materials Required

sheet of newspaper,
preferably a multicolored comic page
tape
scissors

Directions

1. Square off your page (see "How-to Hints"). Designate each corner as A, B, C, or D.
2. Fold in half, creating a triangle. Place the triangle with corner C pointing toward you. Put an E in the exact middle of the area A–B.
3. Fold A down to C. Do the same with B. Now C is covered by B and A. Notice that the shape is once again that of a square.
4. Fold points A, B, and C up and toward spot marked E. Crease. Fold D in opposite direction but also toward E.
5. Tape to secure. Your hat is ready to be opened and tried on.
6. Make and trim the newspaper hats. Create drums from empty coffee cans. Decorate your bikes and wagons. Have a parade around your house or neighborhood.

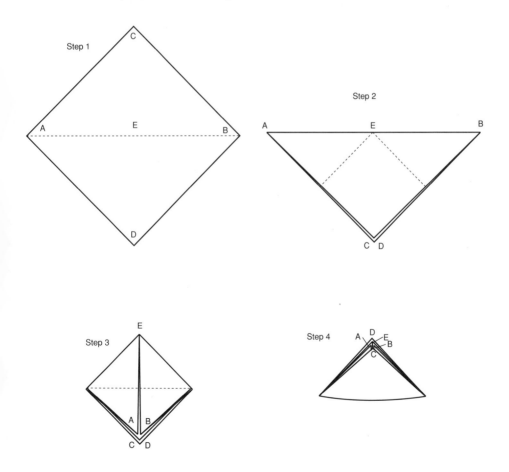

June

Father's Day
Hands
Flag Day
Make a Flag
Frozen Banana Split on a Stick
Jacks
Clover Chain Necklace
Miniature Garden
Paper Cup
Recipe Holder
Red Sails in the Sunset
Send a Letter

Father's Day

In 1909, in Spokane, Washington, Sonora Louise Smart Dodd suggested that a day be designated to honor fathers. Her own father, William Smart, was a Civil War veteran and had been widowed at an early age. Left alone to raise his family of six children, William Smart so impressed his only daughter, Sonora Louise, with his love and conscientious attention to her and her five brothers that she planned a church celebration in June 1910, to pay tribute to him and all fathers.

M. E. Hay, governor of the state of Washington, approved of the idea and declared the third Sunday in June, a date close to William Smart's birthday, as an official day to honor fathers. It was not until 1916 that President Woodrow Wilson proclaimed a national Father's Day.

Hands

Raise your hands, see if they are clean;
They should be the cleanest anyone has seen.
Hold your hands high, make them meet.
Let's see if you washed them—
Are they clean and neat?

Materials Required

8-1/2″ x 11″ sheet of paper or a craft tile or a lid from a
cardboard box, larger in size than the child's hand
crayons
finger paint
laundry marker
stick-on picture hook
pieces of trim, ricrac, lace, or ribbon

Directions

1. Have the child place left or right hand flat on the sheet of paper. Trace around the child's hand. The child might like to draw fingernails, rings, a bracelet, and a watch on the outline of the hand.
2. If using the tile or lid, spread one color of finger paint on a paper plate. With fingers separated, have child place the open hand into the paint and then onto the tile or inside of the lid.
3. Decorate with the trims. Affix hanger on back. Add name and date.
4. For Father's Day, print on the back: "Thanks, Dad, for your helping hand."
5. Wash and dry hands.

Stress the importance of personal hygiene and the washing of hands after each project, after each visit to the bathroom, and before preparing food and eating.

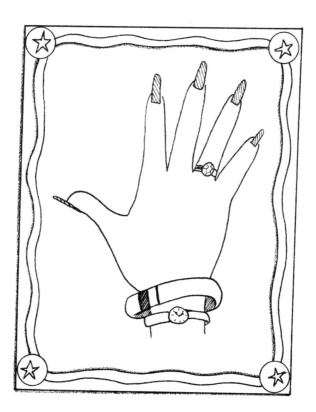

Flag Day

Sara M. Hinson, a schoolteacher in Buffalo, New York, is thought to be the originator of Flag Day. To increase love of country and instill a deep, abiding sense of patriotism in her students, Miss Hinson began school with a salute to the flag and the recitation of the Pledge of Allegiance. The governor of the state of New York issued a proclamation that June 14, 1897, should be celebrated as Flag Day with the national flag flying over all public buildings. Philadelphia, Pennsylvania, also observed Flag Day that year.

June 14 was selected as the date because it was on June 14, 1777, that the Continental Congress passed a law identifying and describing the flag of the United States.

Make a Flag

Pledge of Allegiance

I pledge allegiance to the flag of the United States of America and to the republic for which it stands, one nation under God, indivisible, with liberty and justice for all.

Materials Required

white construction paper
red construction paper
blue construction paper
small gold sticker-type stars
paste or glue

Directions

1. Lay down a sheet of white construction paper in a horizontal position.
2. Cut the red construction paper into appropriate-length strips.
3. Cut and create a blue field.
4. You will need a total of 13 stripes on your flag, with red and white alternating, and a blue field with 50 stars.
5. When you paste the red stripes into position you will automatically have the white stripes show through from the white construction paper. Be sure to start with a red stripe at the top, then white, and alternate, but end with a red stripe as well. It helps to lay the red stripes in place before pasting them down. Remember there are six full-length stripes under the blue field and seven shorter stripes adjacent to the blue field. How many stripes are red? How many are white?

Frozen Banana Split on a Stick

Materials and Ingredients Required

1 cup dry cereal, or cereal-nut crunch
1 small container strawberry-flavored yogurt
3 tablespoons strawberry preserves
3 bananas
plastic bag
rolling pin
wooden popsicle sticks
plate

Directions

1. Put the dry cereal into the plastic bag. Use the rolling pin to crush the cereal.
2. Open and place the yogurt into a pie plate or other suitable dish. Measure and place the preserves in a small dish.
3. Peel bananas and cut in half crosswise. Insert a stick into each banana half.
4. Place the bananas in the plate with the yogurt. Twist and turn the sticks so that each banana half is well coated.
5. Drizzle some preserves on each half.
6. Put bananas in the bag of crushed cereal and coat well.
7. Place prepared bananas in plastic bags or wrap in wax paper and put into the freezer until time to eat and enjoy.

Jacks

Materials Required

6 large-sized jacks
1 small hard rubber ball
a smooth surface

Rules

1. Two players compete if in a tournament. At home, or during play-time, more than two may play.
2. Each draws a number to determine the rotation. The game is played by tossing the jacks from one hand onto the smooth sur-face. The player tries to pick up the jack(s) in proper sequence while the ball is in the air and without touching the other jacks in the process.

3. The player begins by picking up the jacks according to the required sequence: one jack at a time (onesy), two jacks at a time (twosy), three jacks at a time (threesy), and so forth.
4. Jacks must be tossed from one hand only.
5. Only one toss per sequence is allowed, except when jacks are interlocked. Then one additional scramble is permitted.
6. After the jacks have been tossed, the player may not change seated position.

7. The sequence number (4, 5, 6, etc.) of jacks must be taken first. Leftover jacks less than the sequence number are always picked up last.
8. Jacks may be passed from the hand in which the jacks are picked up to the other.
9. "King" (one jack on top of the other) means nothing. If king occurs after jacks have been tossed twice in onesy, the player must try to pick up one jack without touching or moving the other.
10. Bounce the ball after each sequence. Once after onesy, twice after twosy, three times after threesy, etc. Some communities have the player bounce the ball as described but before each sequence. Ball is not to be caught between the required bounces at this time.
11. When player commits an error or a miss, play moves to the next player.

Clover Chain Necklace

Materials Required

long-stemmed clovers

Directions

1. Collect long-stemmed clovers.
2. Tie the stem of the first clover around the flower portion of the second clover. Repeat until the clover chain is the desired length.
3. Tie the last clover stem to the first to complete the necklace.
4. If preferred, use field daisies instead of clover. With your thumbnail make a slit in the stem of each daisy. Slip the next one through.

Miniature Garden

June is the perfect time to be outdoors and enjoy God's gifts of nature. Use some of its treasures to create a bit of your own beauty.

Materials Required

an aluminum pie plate
moss
small rocks or pebbles
small flowers
twigs
miniature figures or toy people

Directions

1. Sprinkle water in the bottom of the pie plate and place the moss over it.
2. Carefully arrange the tiny rocks and small flowers in the aluminum pie plate. Small twigs can serve as trees in your very own special garden.
3. Add miniature figures or toy people.
4. Tomorrow or next week change the flowers and toys and create a new garden.

Paper Cup

Are you thirsty? Are you traveling? Are you camping or at a picnic with no clean cups available? Quickly make one for yourself.

Materials Required

sheets of clean paper
(do not use newspaper or printed pages)
You will need one sheet for each cup.

Directions

1. Square off the paper. Remember to look in the "How-to Hints" section.

2. Designate each corner of your page A B C or D.
3. Fold your square page in half, forming a triangle, with corner B folded up to corner D. Crease your paper. Fold corner A over and to a point about halfway between B and C.
4. Fold corner C opposite point A. Crease well. Fold B down and over. Insert it between the folds of paper that make corner C. Fold corner D in the opposite direction and smooth it against the side of the cup. Open your paper cup, and it is ready for use.

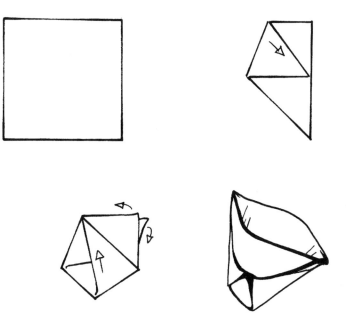

Recipe Holder

Anyone who uses a recipe to cook a favorite dish can certainly use a recipe holder. This makes a delightful gift.

Materials Required

small clay flower pot
piece of styrofoam
few small plastic or silk flowers
ribbon or ricrac
plastic picnic fork
recipe card

Directions

1. Decorate the top edge of the flower pot with ricrac or ribbon.
2. Cut and place a piece of styrofoam into the bottom of the flower pot. Press to fit snugly.

3. Insert some small plastic or silk flowers into the styrofoam.
4. Insert a plastic picnic fork, with tines on top. Place the recipe card between the tines of the fork.

Red Sails in the Sunset

Red sky at night, sailor's delight;
Red sky in the morning, sailor take warning.
Folklore

Long before there were modern means to predict the weather, sailors could tell by the color of the skies what they would face weatherwise the next day. Early morning red skies meant a storm was on the way. Evening red skies indicated smooth sailing. Often in early days the departure of a ship was based on the weather. Today you can make your own sailboat no matter what the weather.

Materials Required

wax paper or freezer paper
permanent markers
bar of soap that floats
drinking straw
tape
nail

Directions

1. Cut out square, rectangular, or triangular shaped sails from the wax paper and decorate with the markers.
2. Affix the sails to the straw with tape, leaving 1" of straw at the base.
3. Bore a small hole into the top of the soap with a nail.
4. Insert the base of the straw into the hole in the center of the bar of soap. It will be easier to insert if the top of the soap is dampened a little. The adult is the captain, guarding carefully the young navigator as the boats are set sailing in the tub or wading pool.

Send a Letter

Encourage the child to write a letter or postcard to himself or herself, or have several children send letters to each other. Show the children the correct way to address the envelope. Add the proper postage stamp. Go to the post office or mailbox and mail the letters. The child will be delighted to receive mail just like Mom and Dad.

Child's Name
1010 Lake Court
City, State, Zip

Stamp
goes
here

Miss Jane Doe
333 Apple Drive
Hometown, State
Zip

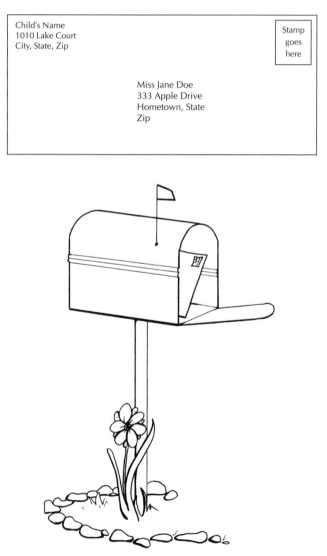

July

Independence Day: The Fourth of July
Fun on Stilts
Patriotic Parade
Clothespin-Doll Family
Constellation Gazer
Fractions
Brown-Bag Target Toss
Rhythm Shakers
Tambourine
Miniature-Golf Course
Silly Sandwiches
Vacation Bingo

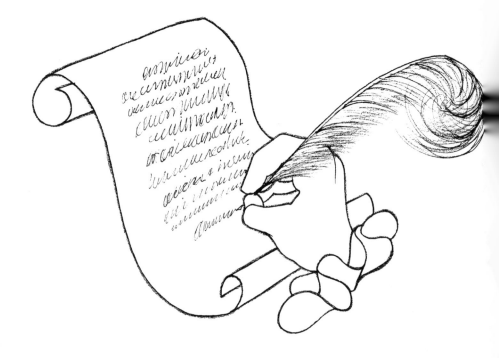

Independence Day: The Fourth of July

We celebrate Independence Day because it is the birthday of our nation. The Declaration of Independence was adopted on July 4, 1776. It is a national holiday celebrated in every state in the union.

On June 11, 1776, the Continental Congress appointed by ballot a committee to prepare a document that declared the thirteen colonies independent of England's rule. Thomas Jefferson wrote the declaration, and after a very few changes by John Adams and Benjamin Franklin, it was put before Congress on June 28, 1776, and adopted July 4, 1776. This famous writing begins with these words: "When, in the course of human events, it becomes necessary for one people to dissolve the political bands which have connected them with another, . . ."

Fun on Stilts

Parades are always taking place in the month of July. Plan one of your own—complete with a stilt walker.

Materials Required

2 large empty fruit juice cans, 46-oz. size
heavy string or clothesline
pry-type bottle or can opener

Directions

1. Depending on the age of the youngsters, let them make or have them assist you in making stilts.
2. Use empty juice cans of equal size and shape. Remove the labels and punch holes opposite each other on the sides of the cans and on top.
3. Insert heavy string through the holes and knot. Keep the lengths equal for both cans, and long enough so the user can hold the strings while standing on top of the cans.
4. Hold the ropes while keeping a can on each foot. The young one will be walking on the stilts with your assistance.

Patriotic Parade

Directions

1. Make and trim paper hats from newspaper.
2. Create drums from empty cylindrical-shaped boxes or empty plastic ice cream containers.
3. Decorate bikes and wagons.
4. Ask for volunteers to walk on stilts.
5. Plan a parade around your house or neighborhood.
6. Get out your flag. Carry it with respect.

Clothespin-Doll Family

Materials Required

clothespins (wooden, not spring clip)
scraps of yarn, fabrics
markers, paints, or crayons
cardboard
imagination

Directions

1. Paint or color faces on the heads of the clothespins.
2. Decorate with yarn for the hair, paper and fabric scraps for the clothes.
3. Cut a piece of cardboard 4" x 2". Bend in half. Insert between the prongs or the clothespins to help your dolls stand.

Constellation Gazer

A constellation is a specific grouping of stars to which a special name has been given. One of the most famous constellations is called Ursa Major. You know it as "The Big Dipper."

Did you know that no matter what the weather or season or time of day, you can view different constellations? You can, by creating your very own and showing them in your home.

Materials Required

an empty potato chip or
snack canister—cylindrical in shape
scissors
thin pieces of cardboard
black construction paper
pencil
nail
tape
markers
flashlight

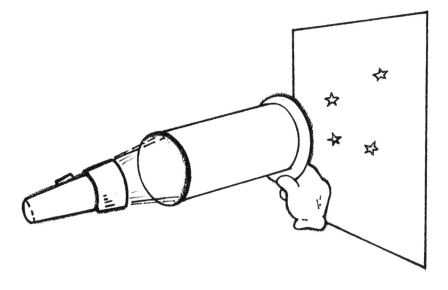

Directions

1. Remove the ends of the container. Use the plastic lid from the container to draw circles on the thin cardboard. Cut them out but cut them larger than the circle pattern.
2. In an encyclopedia find drawings of the constellations or use the drawings of constellations in the back of this book (pp. 229–30). Copy them onto the pieces of circled cardboard.
3. With the nail, carefully poke holes at each designated pencil mark so that you have recreated the various constellations. Remember: one constellation to a circle. Identify each constellation by printing its name on the circle.
4. Tape the black construction paper onto the wall. Turn off the lights. Hold a constellation pattern against the bottom of the container.
5. Shine the flashlight in the opposite end. Hold it so that the constellation appears on the black paper on the wall.
6. As you become familiar with the various constellations, try to find them in the sky on a clear night.

Fractions

A fraction is a mathematical term referring to a number of equal parts of a whole or unit. It is never too early to learn about fractions. They are easy to include in daily activities, especially at lunchtime or snacktime.

Materials Required

pizza
pie
waffles
toast
oranges

Directions

1. Cut the toast or waffle into two pieces—halves, or into four pieces—fourths.

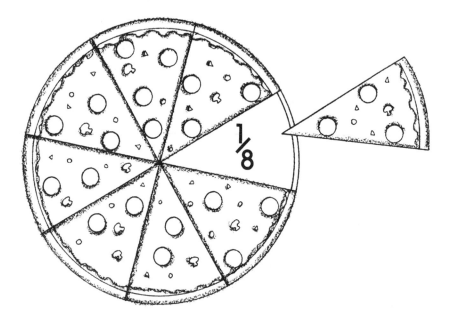

2. A pie or pizza can be cut into sixths or eighths, and it becomes apparent that half a pie is the same as three-sixths or four-eighths.
3. An orange cut in half or in segments can also be used to demonstrate fractions long before math is introduced in a classroom setting.

Brown-Bag Target Toss

Develop accuracy and skill and have some fun-filled hours all at the same time.

Materials Required

2 or 3 brown paper grocery bags
aluminum foil
round objects to use as patterns for target holes
markers
tape
ruler
pencil
stapler
scissors

Directions

1. Draw four circular targets onto a flattened brown bag. Trace different-sized round objects onto the bag. Put either 5, 10, or 15 above the various openings depending upon the size—the smaller the opening the larger the number.
2. Insert the second unmarked brown bag inside of the marked one. Carefully with the scissors cut out the holes through only the top-side of both bags. An adult should supervise or assist a young child.
3. For support, roll the tops of the bags down about an inch or so. Fold again and staple the fold in place.

4. Squeeze a few pieces of various lengths of aluminum foil into different-sized balls.
5. Stand your target bag up and position yourself about 3 feet from it (closer or farther depending on the age of the players). Throw the balls at the target, aiming for the holes. Keep score. Highest score wins.
6. When finished playing, store the foil balls inside the bags so they don't get lost.

Rhythm Shakers

Rhythm is a term used in music for the flow of sound marked by identifiable beats at regular and repeated intervals. Make your own instrument and play your own tune with your own rhythmic beat.

Materials Required

empty and rinsed 6-oz. or 12-oz. frozen orange juice cans
several hard beans, rice, or pebbles
construction paper
pencil
masking tape
paste
scissors

Directions

1. Using the end of the can as a guide, draw a circle on the construction paper and cut the circle from the paper.
2. Drop the beans, rice, or pebbles into the empty can.
3. Tape the circle onto the opened end to prevent the noise makers from falling out. Warn the little ones that the beans belong in the can, not in the mouth or ears.
4. Decorate the outside of the can with construction paper and designs. Your shaker is ready to add some rhythm to the day.
5. To make another sound, place a piece of tissue paper over a clean comb and hum into it. Accompany the musicians playing the shakers and the tambourine (next page).

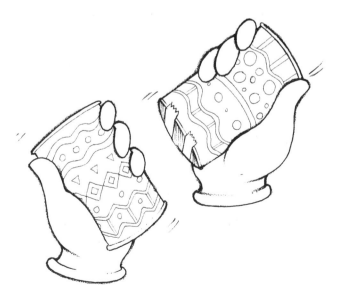

Tambourine

Music and rhythm add to the enjoyment of a moment, a day, and a lifetime. It's good to start appreciating music in a basic form early in life. So have fun making your own source of music and rhythm.

Materials Required

2 disposable aluminum pie plates
yarn or heavy twine
pebbles
metal washers
masking tape
pipe cleaners or twisties
paper punch

Directions

1. Align the two plates one on top of the other with the insides facing each other.
2. Place the pebbles inside. Tape the plates together.
3. Punch through both plates. Insert the twisty or pipe cleaner to secure the plates in the same position.

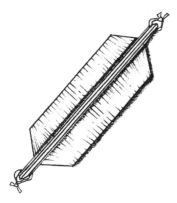
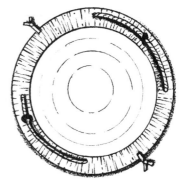

4. Punch at intervals around the edges. Thread the yarn or twine in and out of the holes. At 3, 6, 9, and 12 o'clock on the plate, weave into the twine a pair of metal washers. Tie all securely.

5. Get the beat! Play your tambourine—thump it, shake it.

Miniature-Golf Course

Create one in your own backyard.

Materials Required

empty, clean tin cans—open on one end
empty, clean, large-size (46-oz.) juice cans—open on
both ends
a few logs, stones, bricks, planks
sand
sticks with "flags" numbering the holes
a putter golf club
golf balls (regular or plastic)

Directions

1. Design your course according to your family's skill and the ages of your family members. It helps to have the grass short.
2. The cans, opened on one end only, become the golf holes.
3. The fruit juice cans become the tunnels through which golf balls must pass on the way to the different holes.
4. Make your course as easy or as difficult, as long or as short, as you desire.
5. Number the holes. If you created only three, play each one three times.
6. Keep score. Try for a hole-in-one. Lowest score wins.

Silly Sandwiches

A child is never too young to learn about squares, triangles, and circles—especially when the learning is done in a fun way and food is involved.

Materials Required

peanut-butter-and-jelly sandwiches
bologna sandwiches
open-faced melted-cheese sandwiches

Directions

1. Remove the crusts from the sandwich.
2. With a knife cut the sandwich in half, creating two rectangles.
3. Cut one of the rectangles in half again (from bottom right corner to upper left corner) creating two triangles. Squares or circles can be cut and various designs made such as a clown face, a house, or a flower.
4. Use carrot strips for hair or whiskers, olives or raisins for eyes, cherries for mouth, and celery pieces for tails or ears.

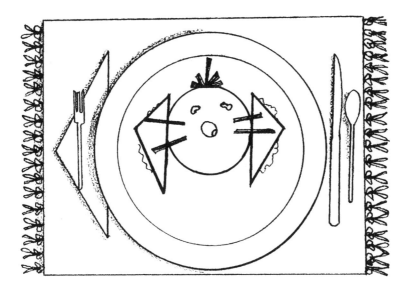

Use your imagination and enjoy fun and healthy eating.

Vacation Bingo

Make your own bingo cards. Use a piece of construction paper for each card or player. Create a suitable number of individual squares. List objects that you are apt to see as you are driving on your vacation such as a barn, clock, cornfield, cow, flag, horse, flower, etc. Print the word for one object in each block. Make sure each card has some different objects. Tape a sheet of thin plastic over the top of each card or cover with clear contact paper. Use a washable marker for each player to X the item when spotted on the drive. First person with card completed is the winner.

This can be adapted for playing at home by creating cards on which pictures from magazines are pasted, one in each square. One marker at a time is drawn and the person who calls out first that it is on his or her bingo card is given the marker to cover the appropriate square. With the name of the object printed on the markers drawn and then given as covers, you'll be surprised at the skill children develop for spelling and alphabet recognition. This can be as basic as the ABCs or words such as *apple, dog, girl,* or *boy.*

August

Checkers

The game of checkers is known as "draughts" in England. The game has been played in Europe since the sixteenth century and was a popular pastime in ancient civilizations. In very early days, stones were used. You can make your own game of checkers.

Materials Required

12 red bottle caps
12 black bottle caps
markers
square piece of cardboard
ruler

Directions

1. Save bottle caps. If possible, have two distinct colors. If not possible, use marker to color 12 black and 12 red.
2. Make a checkerboard from a square piece of cardboard. You can be as fancy as you wish, using colored squares of paper or crayoning in the individual squares on your board. Just make sure that you have 64 squares and alternate the colors, using black and white. The corner end square on each player's right must be white. The corner square on each player's left must be black.
3. The object of the games is to capture all of your opponent's "men" or caps, or block them so they cannot be moved.
4. Each player places 12 red or black checkers (bottle caps) on the dark squares of the first three rows on opposite ends of the board.

5. The first move must be made by the person having the black men. The winner of the previous game has the choice of taking red or black. Toss a coin to determine who has red and black for the first game.

6. The move must be a diagonal step forward, one square at a time. If a hostile man is blocking, and if the square beyond him is vacant, the man must be captured by jumping over him to the vacant square. The process is repeated if a second man is blocking the next square and the square beyond him is vacant. Captured men are removed from the board.

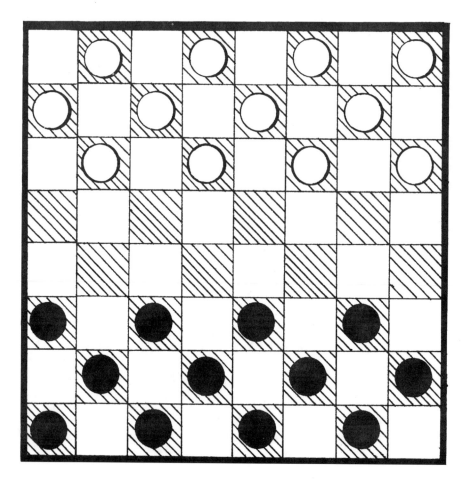

Checkers Tournament

1. The board shall be placed so that the bottom corner square on the left hand shall be black.

2. All men (black and red) should be placed on the 12 black squares closest to the respective players. The first move must be made by the person having the black men (the winner to have the choice of taking black or red for the second game). Toss a coin to determine which player should have black men for first game.

3. The move of the checker men is a diagonal step forward, one square at a time. If a hostile man is in his way and if the square beyond the hostile man is vacant, he must capture him by jumping over him on the vacant square, and he must continue capturing from the square on which he lands as long as this is possible according to the above rule. Captured men are removed from the board.

4. If a man reaches the opposite edge of the board, he automatically becomes a "king" and must be "crowned" by the opponent, who must place another man on top of him. A king may move and capture backward as well as forward. A man who reaches the "king row" in capturing cannot, however, continue capturing on the same move with the newly made king.

5. A player must always take a jump. If he fails to do so, a player may ask the opponent to retract his move and to make the capture.

6. When a player touches a checker, he must move that man. A move is completed when the fingers leave the checker being moved.

7. If a player refuses to move within three minutes, having been given sufficient warning, he forfeits the game to his opponent. The warning is to be given after one and a half minutes or original three minutes.

8. If a stalemate occurs, the game is called a tie, and another game is started.

Clothespin Challenge and Hunt

Clothespins are handy to have around the house, and add to the fun of playtime. Here's a game that will help youngsters develop eye-hand coordination: the clothespin challenge.

Materials Required

10 wooden clip clothespins
empty and cleaned half-gallon cardboard milk or
fruit juice container

Directions

1. Rinse out the empty container and let it dry.
2. Open the cardboard top as wide as possible and place it on the floor.

3. Have the child kneel on a chair or stand tall. The child will hold a clothespin in one hand and, using the tip of child's nose as starting point, drop the pin toward the open container.
4. The object is to see how many pins can be dropped into the container.
5. Another use of clothespins can take place on a nice day outdoors. Clip the pins to bushes, tree branches, outdoor furniture, etc. The children must see who can locate the most clips in a given time.

Scavenger Hunt

Plan a summertime scavenger hunt outdoors with items based on the ages of the group and the season.

Directions

1. Create teams or play individually. Provide each player with the identical list of items and a bag in which to place the located items.
2. Each team sets out to locate the listed items. The first team to collect all the items—or the team that has the most items within a designated time period—wins.

Sample List

bottle cap
snail's shell
flat, white rock
four-leaf clover
wildflower or dandelion
maple leaf
pinecone
an item that is red, white, and blue

Riddle Dee Diddle: Colors

No special materials or items are needed to play this game. Anywhere, anytime is fine. Traveling in a car, waiting for mom or dad to arrive home, sitting in a doctor's or dentist's office are all suitable locations to play.

Directions

1. One person designates a mystery item and recites this jingle:

> Riddle dee diddle, hi dee dee,
> I see something you don't see,
> And the color is————.

2. The rest of the group takes turns trying to guess what the item is. Whoever "finds" the item first gets to pick the next one.
3. Your own rules should apply. For example, the item being guessed must be inside the car or in a particular room. If the group is in the kitchen, the color could be red and the mystery item could be an apple.

Rose Potpourri

A fun-to-make and nostalgic gift to receive is a sachet or jar filled with rose potpourri.

Materials Required

6 cups of dried rose petals
1/2 cup dried mint flakes
1/2 teaspoon ground cloves
1/2 teaspoon ground cinnamon
1/2 teaspoon ground allspice
1-1/2 tablespoons orris root
(available from a drugstore)

Directions

1. Save the freshest petals from a variety of fragrant roses, although the same kind and color will also serve the purpose.
2. Separate the petals and spread only the petals in a single layer in the lid of a shallow cardboard box.
3. Place in a dry, shady spot for a few days until they are completely dried.
4. Combine the spices and orris root in a clean container with a lid. Add the rose petals to the spice mixture. Mix well. If you have an oil-based fragrance, add a few drops; although it is not essential, it will strengthen the fragrant aroma. Cover tightly.
5. Set this aside for a month, but remember to shake or stir every few days. Keep the container covered between stirrings.
6. After a month, divide the potpourri into amounts appropriate for individual net sachet bags or small containers. Tie each with a pretty ribbon.

Special Stack Snack

Little ones—and big ones, too—enjoy making and eating this stack snack.

Ingredients and Materials Required

3 cups dry cereal flakes
1/2 cup light corn syrup
1/2 cup granulated sugar
3/4 cup peanut butter
1/2 cup butterscotch chips
1/2 cup chocolate chips
tray or cookie sheet with wax paper on it
mixing bowl and spoon
measuring cups
two different-sized saucepans

Directions

1. Adult supervision is needed. Always wash hands before and after cooking.
2. Assemble everything that will be used.
3. Measure the cereal into a large mixing bowl.
4. Place the syrup, sugar, and peanut butter in heat-proof pan. With adult supervision, place the pan and the contents on the stove over low heat until the ingredients are melted. Remove from stove.
5. Pour over the cereal and mix well by using a large mixing spoon.
6. Drop by spoonfuls onto the wax paper.
7. Put the dirty bowl and pan in the sink and add water to soak.
8. Place a smaller pan on low heat, and add the butterscotch and chocolate chips. Carefully stir until melted. If available, you may prefer using a double boiler or a microwave oven to prevent chips from scorching; however, if carefully watched a pan on low heat will work satisfactorily.
9. Remove from stove. Drop a small dollop of this mixture on top of each stack.
10. These snacks are ready to be eaten and enjoyed. Before snacking, clean up the work area.

Spool Artwork

Did you think that spools were made to only hold thread? When they are empty, use them to create designs.

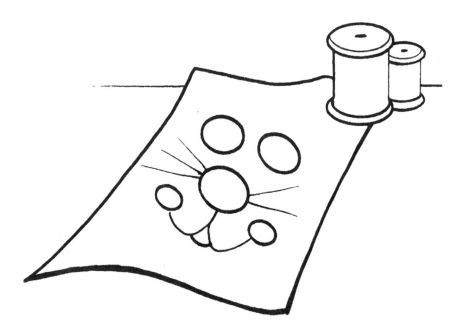

Materials Required

empty spools of various sizes
crayons, markers, colored pencils
sheets of paper
imagination

Directions

1. Collect the empty spools.
2. Carefully draw around one or more spools with pencil or crayon.
3. Add colored lines, dots, or dashes to create faces, animals, and designs.

Super Bubbles

Bubbles can be a source of joy and fun for "kids" of all ages. Remember blowing bubbles as a child with a bubble wand? Today, share that fun by creating super bubbles.

Materials Required

pipe cleaners
pie tin
soap solution (recipe below)

Directions

1. Mix and shake 1 cup dishwashing liquid, 3 cups water, and 3/8 cup light corn syrup. Let stand to settle 4 hours before first use. Store in covered container.
2. Wrap the pipe cleaner around a circular object (a soft-drink can will work nicely) and twist the ends together to form a circle with a stem.
3. Mix the bubble solution and pour into a pie tin.
4. Dip the circle pipe cleaner into the solution and gently blow to create extra-large "super bubbles." If you like, use two pipe cleaners to make an even bigger circle and bigger bubbles.
5. This is best done outdoors on a fairly calm day. You may not want bubble residue on floors and furniture.

Water Balloons and Watermelon

Materials Required

balloons
water
paper plates, napkins
icy cold watermelon

On a hot summer's day, have the young ones put on their bathing suits. Prepare a supply of balloons filled with water. Have a watermelon iced and waiting. Spread some beach towels on the lawn in a shady spot. Enjoy a water balloon toss. While the young ones dry off on the towels, begin serving slices of the ice-cold watermelon. Save some of the seeds. They can be dried and later glued on construction paper for an art project.

Rules for a Balloon Toss

Separate the group into two parallel lines, facing each other. One line will be holding the balloons. Toss the balloon to your "partner" in the other line. If the partner catches it, he or she takes one step back and then tosses back to his or her partner. If the balloon is dropped and/or breaks, that pair is out. Repeat this process until only one pair remains. They are the winners!

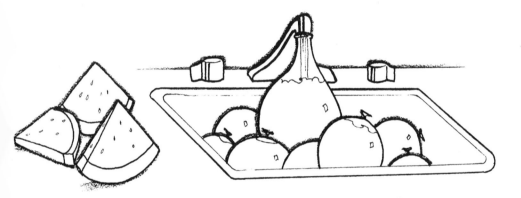

September

Labor Day

The first Monday in September is generally observed in the United States and Canada as a "holiday for labor." At the beginning of the nineteenth century, conditions for a person working in a factory or in a mine were very different from what we know today. Long hours, unpleasant conditions, and unfair pay were routine rather than the exception. In 1830 many unions were being formed, and a great satisfaction was felt when in 1840 President Martin Van Buren ordered a ten-hour maximum for a working day on all government projects, with no reduction in wages. In 1869 Uriah S. Stephens, a tailor in Philadelphia, founded a union named the Noble Order of the Knights of Labor that was open to all workers. It favored an eight-hour working day and equal pay for equal work done by women.

In 1882 Peter J. McGuire, founder of a labor union called the United Brotherhood of Carpenters and Joiners of America, proposed that one day a year be designated as Labor Day, a holiday for the laboring classes. He persuaded the Central Labor Union of New York City to hold the first Labor Day parade on September 5, 1882.

Bird Feeder

Materials Required

an empty coffee can with a removable lid
2 aluminum pie plates
heavy cord
pry-type can opener
hammer and nail
birdseed

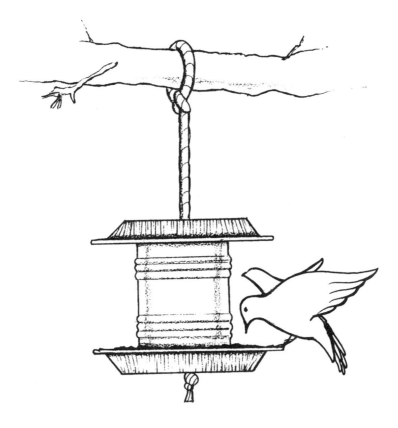

Directions

1. With the can opener make holes at intervals around the bottom edge of the can and then remove the ends of the coffee can.

2. Poke a hole in the center of each of the two pie plates, large enough for the string to fit through.

3. Tie a large, secure knot in the end of the string and thread the string through the bottom of the one pie plate, through the can, and then through the hole in the inside of the other pie plate. Tie a strong knot 12 inches above the top plate by which you can hang the feeder on a tree branch safe from squirrels and cats.

4. Lift the top pie plate to fill the can with birdseed.

5. The seed will pour out a little at a time to feed the hungry birds.

Carton Fun

With the older children back in school, the younger ones are looking for extra things to do.

Directions

1. For very young children, create a train from large, empty cartons. Place several large boxes in a row, designating the first one as the engine and ending with the last as the caboose.
2. Turn a really large carton upside down and with a permanent marker create a "stove top" with large circles for burners, small ones for knobs, designs for panels, buttons, etc.
3. The same can be done for a "refrigerator" made from a large carton.
4. Imagination and ingenuity are limitless.

Crunchy and Crispy Confections

Ingredients Required and Materials

1 package marshmallows (approx. 40 regular size or
4 cups miniature marshmallows)
1/4 cup margarine
6 cups oven-toasted rice cereal
1/2 teaspoon vanilla extract
large wooden spoon
buttered 9" x 13" pan
large saucepan or microwave-safe mixing bowl

Directions

1. Adult supervision is required.
2. Melt margarine in large saucepan over very low heat.
3. Add marshmallows and stir until melted. Remove from heat. Add the vanilla extract.
4. Add the cereal. Stir until well coated.
5. Use large, wooden, buttered spoon to spread mixture into the 9" x 13" pan. With wax paper or a plastic sandwich bag on your hand, press the mixture evenly in the pan.
6. Cut into squares and triangles when cool.
7. This can be made in a microwave oven by placing margarine and marshmallows in a microwave-safe mixing bowl and microwaving on high for 1-1/2 minutes. Stir. Rotate bowl. Microwave another 1-1/2 minutes. Stir until smooth. Add vanilla extract. Add cereal. Stir until well coated. Follow steps 5 and 6.

Dollhouse

Materials Required

empty large detergent box
tape
cardboard
scraps of material, contact paper, wallpaper samples
water colors
old magazine with suitable photos of
appropriate furniture, artwork, refrigerator, stove, etc.
markers
scissors
ruler

Directions

1. Adult assistance is required.
2. Stand the box upright. Brush out any remaining detergent particles.
3. Cut out one side of the box.
4. Measure the cardboard and create dividers that will be used to separate box into two floors and also divide it into separate rooms. Tape into place.
5. With the water colors paint these pieces the colors of your choice.
6. If desired, brown grocery sacks or contact paper or wrapping paper can be affixed to the outside of the box.
7. Decide where the windows should be located, and with the marker draw them or paste pictures of some from an old magazine. Curtains, drapes, and rugs can be either crayoned or pasted on by using scraps of material.
8. Flower boxes or pictures of flowers growing add a nice touch.

The dollhouse is ready for new occupants. What about your doll family or clothespin-doll family? Are they house hunting?

Drop-and-Blot Designs

Materials Required

water paints or finger paints or few drops of food coloring
sheets of paper
work cloth or old newspaper

Directions

1. Spread the cloth at your work spot.
2. Fold a sheet of paper in half, creating a sharp crease in the paper, and open.

3. Place one drop of color in the center of the crease. Again fold the paper. With your finger rub in several directions over the spot where you have placed the drop of color.
4. Open the paper and decide what the design looks like. A butterfly? A flower? What?
5. Do it again and this time add more drops of color. With crayons or markers add finishing details.

6. Try this project with various types of paper—notebook paper, cardboard, construction paper, paper towels. See what happens. Some types of paper, especially paper towels, are more absorbent than others.

Pomanders

A pomander is an old-fashioned air freshener. It also is a gift that is useful, practical, fragrant, and fun to make. The recipient will be pleased with the fragrance and will hang it in a closet or place it in a drawer.

Materials Required

a firm apple, lemon, lime, or orange
package of whole cloves
ground cinnamon
orris root*
an awl, toothpick, or fork with thick tines
scraps of net
ribbon
silk flowers or small decorative items
brown paper lunch bag

Directions

1. Select whichever fruit you prefer. With the awl or fork poke holes in the fruit. These holes do not have to be in consecutive rows but randomly spaced over the entire surface of the fruit.

*Orris root powder may be purchased at any drugstore. It is not essential but helps to preserve the pomanders.

Insert a whole clove into each hole. A very young child will need some help and guidance in poking the holes and inserting the cloves.

2. Measure equal parts of ground cinnamon and orris root into the bag. The amount used will be determined by the number of pomanders you are making.

3. Place the pomanders in the bag. Shake well so that the spices coat the surface of the fruit. Open the end of the bag. Place bag containing spices and the fruit in a dark, dry, and cool area. Permit the fruit to shrink and dry out completely, probably in three weeks. Check at intervals and note how the fruit is becoming hard to the touch. Also, turn the fruit so it dries uniformly.

4. Cut a square of the netting, large enough to encircle the pomander. Pull the sides of the netting up and tie with a piece of ribbon. Add the little flower. Tie securely. Leave a loop long enough to permit hanging in a closet.

School Bus

The bus is coming down the street.
I hold my hand up high.
Oh, driver, stop beside the post
And do not pass me by.

The bus has shiny leather seats
And windows made of glass.
What fun it is to sit inside
And watch the cars go past!
—Author Unknown

Materials Required

empty 64-oz. juice or milk carton
yellow construction paper
crayons
paste

Directions

1. Cover the entire carton with yellow construction paper.
2. Draw in the windows, doors, and wheels. Remember the STOP sign on the side of the bus. Why does the driver activate this sign each time the bus stops for a rider to enter or depart from the bus?
3. Don't forget to draw a driver and the children inside.

Sweet Potato Vine

To appreciate some of the wonders and marvels of nature, try growing a sweet potato or carrot top right in your own kitchen. You will not get more potatoes, but you will get a beautiful vine.

Materials Required

sweet potato
empty, clean, clear plastic container or cup
four toothpicks

Directions

1. Insert the toothpicks, one on each side of the sweet potato so that only the narrow half of the potato will be below the top of the container and the picks will rest on the sides of the container.

2. Pour water into the container until it covers half of the potato. If you have a few stones or marbles, put them in the bottom of the container to weight down the cup before you put in the potato.

3. Place the cup in a cool, somewhat dark corner for a week to 10 days. Do not disturb except to add water, maintaining the water level. After this period of time you should see roots and shoots.

4. Remove the container from the dark area and set in a warm, light spot, preferably a windowsill. Trim off the smallest shoots so that you have only four or five strong, healthy ones.

5. Make sure the potato always has water touching it. Water is essential for the sweet potato's growth. Soon you will have a lovely sweet potato vine.

Teddy-Bed Brick Bookends

How often have you wished for a pair of bookends to support your own books or to give as a gift to a friend or relative?

Materials Required

2 bricks
2 miniature teddy bears
felt material
fabric scraps
fabric glue
ruler
pencil
scissors

Directions

1. Clean the bricks. Let them dry thoroughly.
2. Cover the entire brick with interesting fabric. Glue felt to the bottom. Roll another piece of fabric to look like a tiny pillow and glue in place.

3. Add a small teddy bear or doll with its head resting on the pillow.
4. Add another piece of coordinating fabric as a blanket or coverlet. Glue on some lace.
5. With the material used and the items added to the top, you can match the color scheme of the room where the bookends will be used. For example, for a child's bedroom cover the brick with nursery print fabric; for the kitchen use a checked gingham. If your favorite animal is a cat or dog, use miniatures of those animals rather than a teddy bear.
6. If you decorate only one brick, you have a doorstop. Interesting innovations can be done to add variety to your doorstops and to make them original creations.

Paper-Plate Clock

Materials Required

two 9" white paper plates
crayons or markers
brass paper fastener
ruler
scissors

Directions

1. Mark the face of the clock with the proper numerals. Decorate the outer edge or rim of the plate.
2. On the second plate, measure one hand approximately 3" x 1/2" and the other 2" x 1/2". Color the hands a dark color. Cut the hands out of the plate.
3. Secure the hands with the fastener in the center of the plate on which you have drawn the numerals.

4. Practice telling time. Set the hands at times to eat, take a nap, do a task, go to bed. When the wall clock corresponds to the time set on the paper clock, it's time to get started.

Table-Top Train

Materials Required

1-quart size milk carton
juice container, emptied and cleaned
several boxes of different sizes
construction paper
glue
scissors
markers
cardboard
paper brads
cord

Directions

1. Cover the items to be used with construction paper or suitable colors. A large juice container or a quart size milk container could be a perfect base for the engine. Use an empty toilet tissue roll for the smokestack.

2. An empty tea box will be ideal as the caboose. Cover it with red paper. Glue a smaller empty box (such as the size from an individual bar of soap) to the top of the wrapped tea box. Be sure to cover it with red paper before affixing it to the wrapped tea box. Add a piece of black construction paper for the flat roof.

3. Use various sized and shaped boxes for the rest of the cars.

4. Be sure to punch a hole in the front and rear of each train car and a hole in the rear of the engine and a hole in the front of the caboose for threading a cord through. Be sure to knot the cord.

5. Using the closed end of a small paper cup as a guide, trace circles on a piece of cardboard. Create enough wheels for your train and cars. Cut them out and attach the wheels with the paper brads.

All aboard!

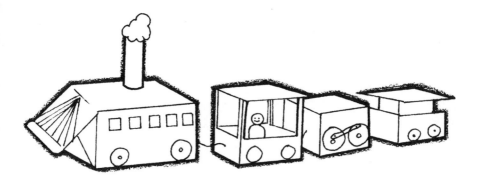

October

Card-Table Clubhouse

A rainy day is the perfect time to create an indoor clubhouse. It's easy to do, and it provides hours of fun.

Materials Required

card table
old sheet or old tablecloth
markers
black crayon
yardstick
safety pins
Velcro patches
scissors (pinking shears are preferable)

Directions

1. Carefully and evenly drape the sheet over the tabletop. The fabric should cover the entire table and hang evenly to the floor. If necessary, trim some of the fabric.
2. Mark the spots where the sheet touches the corners of the tabletop and mark the center.
3. Use the yardstick to extend the lines so that you have created a pattern as shown: one large square in the center and one square for each side of the house. The corner squares will be cut away. If you like, you can extend the sides by one inch to make a seam to stitch the corners of the house shut. Or you can pin the corners together when complete. If you desire a window or door, now is the time to mark them in. Cut out the pattern, including

doors and windows. Consider gluing a piece of Velcro in upper corner door so that it can be closed.

4. Draw in house number, flowers, shutters, and any other decorative items of your choice on the sheet.

5. Drape the house over the table. Be ready to welcome visitors.

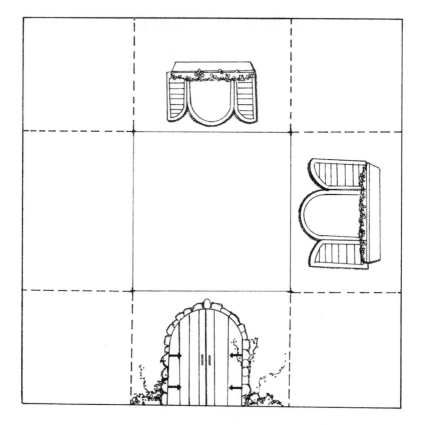

Columbus Day

Columbus Day is a holiday in celebration and commemoration of the discovery of America by Christopher Columbus on October 12, 1492. His crews aboard three small ships—*Nina, Pinta,* and *Santa Maria*—had set sail from Spain with support from Spain's Queen Isabella.

The first celebration of this discovery of America was in New York City on October 12, 1792, three hundred years after the event. The Society of Tammany or Columbian Order arranged it. The 400th anniversary of the discovery of America saw a monument erected at the southwestern entrance to Central Park in New York City and is named Columbus Circle in his honor. On September 30, 1934, President Franklin D. Roosevelt issued a proclamation asking that October 12 be observed as a national holiday. Columbus Day is a holiday that is shared with Central and South America countries, some parts of Canada, Italy, and Spain. Columbus Day 1992 was an exciting time as the 500th anniversary of Columbus' voyage and discovery of America was celebrated.

Felt Fun

Feeling frivolous? Fashion favorite, fancy, fabric figures for family fun. Fundamental, functional, fascinating!

Materials Required

different colors of felt
scissors
shoe box
glue

Directions

1. Cover the lid of the empty shoe box with black felt.
2. Cut shapes such as circles, squares, triangles, rectangles. Keep these shapes inside the shoe box. Use different colors and sizes.
3. Create patterns, designs, and scenes on the covered lid. The felt pieces will stick to the felt cover.
4. Remove the design when satisfied with it, and then make a new one.

Friendly Spider

A teensie weensie spider
Crawled up the water spout.
Down came the rain
And washed the spider out.
Out came the sun
And dried up all the rain,
And the teensie weensie spider
Climbed up the spout again.

—Traditional

Materials Required

cardboard
thumbtacks
thread

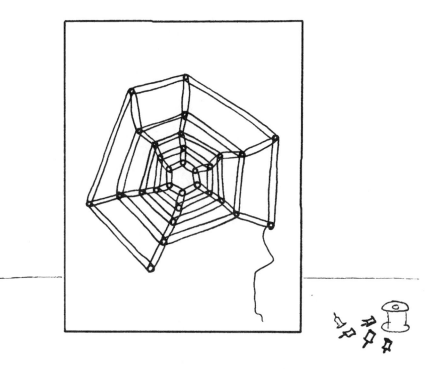

Directions

1. Make a spider web for Halloween by creating a weaving board using a piece of cardboard with thumbtacks placed as in the diagram.
2. Use black thread or black string for your web.
3. Recite the rhyme, using appropriate motions.

Friendship Tea

On a chilly night, a cup of hot friendship tea helps to warm a person. The warmth it creates is outdone only by the warmth of the heart when friendship tea is given as a gift.

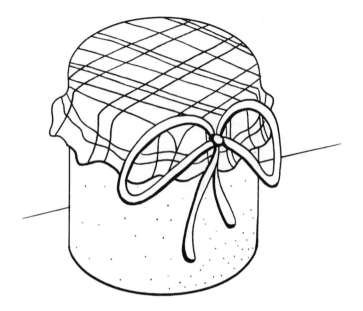

Ingredients

2 cups powdered orange breakfast-drink mix
3/4 cup instant tea
3-oz. instant lemonade mix
1 cup sugar
1-1/2 teaspoons ground cloves
2 teaspoons ground cinnamon

Directions

1. Mix all the ingredients together in large mixing bowl. Blend well.
2. Pour into gift jars (emptied and cleaned baby food or preserves jars will do nicely).
3. Add a piece of checked or printed material to the lid and tie with a piece of yarn.
4. Attach a label with directions for using: To serve add 2–3 tea-spoons of mixture to one cup of hot water.

Satisfaction for the giver and enjoyment for the recipient!

Halloween

Halloween occurs on October 31, which coincides with the time of the ancient Druids' autumn celebration. It is also the time of the ancient Roman festival in honor of Pomona, their mythological goddess of fruit and gardens. Following the spread of Christianity in Europe, November 1 was designated as a day for honoring all saints, a hallowed day. The evening before that day was called Hallowe'en, meaning the "Holy Eve of All-Saints Day," a night when the pagan religions in Europe had ceremonies that made people think goblins and spooks were out and about. The pumpkin lanterns on Halloween are used in imitation of evil spirits associated with the harvest festival of the ancient Druids.

Later in Europe and in the days of the settlement of the United States, Halloween became merely a time of parties and pranks, especially for children.

Great Goody Ghost

Ghosts, goblins, and witches are associated with Halloween. Make your own miniature ghosts as favors for a Halloween party or for a special treat for the members of your family.

Materials Required

white facial tissues
crayons
orange or black thin yarn
small, round-shaped children's lollipops

Directions

1. Count out equal amounts of lollipops and tissues for the number of goody ghosts you wish to make. Place a lollipop inside each tissue.

2. Tie the orange or black yarn at the base of the candy. With your crayons create eyes.

3. Your goody ghosts are ready. They won't fly and they won't scare anyone, but each recipient will enjoy receiving and eating one!

Masks from Paper Plates

Masks, worn to disguise or to protect the face, have been used since time began. Primitive people used masks to impersonate supernatural beings or animals in religious ceremonies. Native American dancers used masks to ward off evil spirits. Asian actors and actresses use masks in their dramatic presentations. Halloweeners enjoy wearing masks for fun.

Materials Required

paper plate
pencil or markers
scissors
ribbon
stapler
yarn, if desired
pipe cleaners

Directions

1. Hold the eating surface of the plate to the face of the child. Gently mark the plate where the eyes, nose, and mouth will be. Move the plate away from the child's face.
2. Cut out the eye area, leaving the top portion attached to be decorated as eyelashes. Color this part black and cut into small slits. Feather back.
3. Cut out the nose but leave it attached at the top near the eyes. Also cut out the mouth area.
4. Decorate the mask. Draw in the lips, hair, etc. If you desire, glue yarn on for the hair. Try creating animals, monsters, or funny faces.
5. Poke a small hole on each side of the mask and attach pipe cleaners. Fold the pipe cleaners behind the ears—like eyeglasses—to hold the mask on the face.

Paper-Cup-and-Tube Game

Develop eye-hand coordination by using the cup-and-tube game.

Materials Required

8-oz. plastic cup or empty yogurt container
cardboard tube from roll of paper towels
a 24" shoelace of any color, or string
tape
ruler
scissors

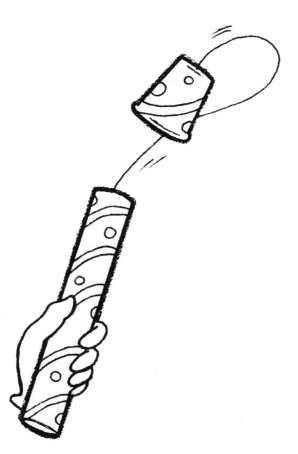

Directions

1. Measure and cut a 24" piece of string and tie a small knot at each end.
2. Securely tape one end of the string about 2" down from the end of the tube. Tape the other end to the center of the bottom of the cup. Decorate the tube with crayons, markers, or stickers if desired.
3. Hold the tube at the opposite end of where you have taped the string. Count how many times you can flip the cup and have it land on top of the tube. Score one point each time you are successful in a specified number of tries per turn. Player with high score wins.

Roasted Pumpkin Seeds

Roasting pumpkin seeds is an age-old, autumn tradition. For years families have enjoyed roasted pumpkin seeds as a reward for carving a beautiful or scary jack-o'-lantern.

Materials Required

one fresh pumpkin
knife
colander
skillet
margarine
cookie sheet
paper towels

Directions

1. Adult supervision is necessary for this entire project.
2. After cutting the top off the pumpkin, use a large spoon to reach inside and remove the seeds. They will still have some pulp on them. Put the seeds into the colander and wash well. Drain the seeds on the paper towels. Pat dry. Remove all remnants of pulp.
3. Melt three tablespoons of margarine in a large skillet. Add up to three cups of seeds to the melted margarine in the skillet. Stir gently as you try to move the seeds so that each becomes coated with melted margarine. Sauté about three minutes. If you desire, add a dash of Worcestershire sauce for flavor.
4. Preheat oven to 300 degrees. Have the lightly greased cookie sheet handy. Spread the seeds on the cookie sheet. Bake 25 minutes. Remove and spread on paper towels to cool. Sprinkle a little table or seasoned salt over the seeds. When cool, eat and enjoy.

November

Veterans' Day

November 11 is known as Veterans' Day, but before 1954 it was called Armistice Day. That name originated from the fact that at 11 o'clock on the eleventh day of the eleventh month in 1918 the actual fighting of World War I ceased. An armistice, or truce, was in effect, and the long battle was over! Since that never-to-be-forgotten time in 1918, an Armistice Day has been observed. An Australian journalist named George Honey called for a two-minute silence as the peace treaty was signed. The tradition of "the great silence" continues in these modern times as well, with community celebrations, parades involving veterans of all wars, the displaying of flags, and the decorating of graves of soldiers.

As the United States became involved in additional wars, Armistice Day was officially renamed Veterans' Day in 1954. Veterans' Day pays tribute to all service people and the brave men and women who defended our nation in World War I, World War II, the Korean War, the Vietnam War, and the Persian Gulf War.

Butter from Cream

Ingredients and Materials Required

2 cups whipping cream
1/4 teaspoon salt
5–6 ice cubes
clean quart-size jar with screw-top lid
medium-size mixing bowl chilled
container to store the butter

Directions

1. Place the refrigerated cream and the glass jar in a warm spot for approximately 2 to 3 hours.
2. Pour the warm cream into the warmed jar.
3. With the lid tightly screwed, hold the jar securely with one hand on top and one on bottom of the jar. Begin shaking the jar and saying:

> From the cow comes cream,
> From cream comes butter.
> Served on hot biscuits
> Makes appetites flutter.

4. Take turns shaking the jar. Continue to shake the jar for 15 minutes or until the butter gathers into a solid mass.
5. If you have problems getting the butter to hold together, just add a few teaspoons of hot water.
6. Pour off the buttermilk and place the butter ball in the chilled mixing bowl.
7. Wash hands, making sure they are very clean.
8. Add the ice cubes to the mixing bowl. As the cubes melt, with your fingers work the ice water into the butter ball. This will chill the butter, and you can pour off the remaining water and cubes.
9. Add the salt by gently sprinkling it over the butter. Work the salt, again using your fingers, into the butter until the grains of salt dissolve.
10. Shape the butter into desired form.
11. Wrap or place on butter dish and cover. Refrigerate until used.

Cornucopia

A cornucopia can be a small basket or a larger one for a table decoration.

Materials Required

construction paper: any color if for a basket
brown grocery bag or tan construction paper for table
decoration
paste or tape
sticker for decoration

Directions

1. Square the paper to the appropriate size: large for table decoration, smaller for individual baskets.

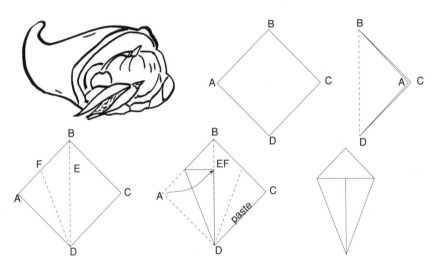

2. Fold the square in half from A to B. Crease the paper from B to D. The folded square now has the shape of a triangle.
3. Open the triangle and then fold both sides toward the center crease (fold along the line from D to F, thus taking A to E).
4. Paste or tape along the edge between D to C. Press DC to the top of DF. For an extra touch for a basket, punch a hole and insert a piece of ribbon.
5. For a table decoration, place some fruit or vegetables in the cornucopia. If using as a favor or basket, fill with candy corn.
6. Remember, you can use tiny ones on your Christmas tree, or in May fill with flowers for May Day or Mother's Day.

Thanksgiving Day

Of all the holidays celebrated in the United States, none is so distinctively "American" as Thanksgiving. The very first Thanksgiving Day in America was celebrated by the Pilgrims in 1621 as they gave thanks to our Creator for the fall harvest and for surviving the treacherous days of starvation and hardships. The feast was held by the colonists and shared with the neighboring Indians. It was the Indians who taught the colonists to raise the corn and pumpkins and to hunt and prepare the wild turkeys.

Soon the custom of celebrating a Thanksgiving Day spread from Plymouth to the other colonies. In 1789, President Washington issued a general Thanksgiving Day proclamation. Through the efforts of Mrs. Sarah Josepha Hale, editor of *Godey's Lady's Book*, Thanksgiving Day became an annual holiday. After twenty years of writing to the presidents, her efforts were rewarded when President Lincoln appointed the last Thursday in November as Thanksgiving Day. In 1939 President Franklin D. Roosevelt proclaimed the third Thursday in November as the national Thanksgiving Day. In 1941, after outcries from traditionalists, Congress and the president agreed to return Thanksgiving Day to the fourth Thursday in November.

Indian Canoe

Indians sit here!

Indians made their canoes by hollowing out tree trunks and then carving them into shape. Once finished, they would use tree sap to coat the wood to keep it from absorbing water. This process could take weeks to complete. But you can make a play canoe in just a few minutes.

Materials Required

1 empty toothpaste box 4.6-oz. size
tan construction paper or paper from a grocery bag
scissors
glue
ruler
pencil
markers
stapler

Directions

1. Draw a pattern, as shown, on the fold of a brown bag. Notice that the depth, length, and width should be large enough to fit the toothpaste box when it is placed inside of the paper.
2. Remove the top side of the toothpaste box.
3. With markers draw a design onto the outer sides of the canoe.
4. Cut out the canoe from the bag. Measure 1" along the length of the fold and crease on both sides, thus creating a well into which the box can fit.
5. Spread glue on the cut-out paper canoe form. Attach to the box.
6. Staple, glue, or tape the ends of the canoe together.

Remember, this canoe is for play, not for floating!

Indian Headdress

The Native Americans have a very proud heritage of honesty, bravery, and love for each other. These are excellent characteristics to share with children.

Materials Required

one grocery bag, light brown in color, or
a strip of tan corrugated paper
two sheets vibrant-colored construction paper, or
two feathers
pencil, crayons, or markers
ruler
scissors
paste

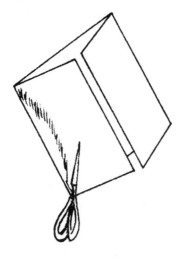

Directions

1. Place opened and smoothed bag on a working surface.
2. Measure and mark 4" from the open end of bag. Mark completely around the top. Cut off this 4" strip.
3. Use a tape measure to determine size of your "Indian's" head. Cut the paper band accordingly but be sure to leave 1" extra paper in the length so that you will have an overlap to staple or glue after folding the band into thirds lengthwise.
4. The band should be approximately 1-1/3" wide and long enough to go around the head with an overlap for gluing or stapling together. Draw an Indian design on the band.

5. Fold the colored construction paper in half. Open the paper, and using the center fold as a guide, fold each end inward so that you have created a page that opens like a shutter. On each fold sketch the outline of half a feather. Cut out the feathers. They should be about 2-3/4" at the widest section and 8-1/2" long. Taper the ends. Do the same with the other colored piece of paper.

6. Snip at intervals along the sides of each feather to create a feathery look.

7. Insert and glue or staple the feathers into the headband at the point of the overlap. An Indian princess wears two feathers in her headdress, while an Indian brave requires only one.

8. Another quick and easy way to make an Indian headdress is to cut a strip of corrugated cardboard approximately 1-1/2" wide and long enough to go around the child's head. Fasten the two ends of the strip together with tape or by stapling. Insert feathers into several of the ridges of the corrugated cardboard or use only one feather.

9. Use a brown grocery bag and create an Indian vest. Don't forget the designs and the fringe.

Indian Village

Materials Required

brown grocery bag
pencil, crayons, or markers
15" round tray
few toothpicks
scissors
tape
stapler
paste

Directions

1. Cut the bottom of the bag so that it will lie flat. If you have made only the headdress use the remaining portion of that bag.
2. With the bag flat on your work space, place the tray on top of the bag and trace around the tray with a pencil.
3. Cut through both layers of the bag and you will have two circles each 15″ in diameter.
4. Fold one circle in half. With the markers decorate the half-circle with Indian designs and figures.
5. Fold the half-circle in half again. Do not crease. Using tape, affix the toothpicks in the center of the straight edge. Fold the ends until the sides meet. Staple together. The edges can be rolled back to create a "flapped" look on the tent. Repeat with the other circle.

Magic Index Card

A clever trick: Can you slip your head through a 5″ x 7″ index card?

Materials Required

5″ x 7″ index card or regular size construction paper
scissors

Directions

1. Fold the card in half lengthwise. Place the folded edge toward you.
2. With the scissors start cutting as follows: Begin your first cut from the folded edge. The next cut begins from the open edge. Alternate cuts at every 1/2″ to 3/4″ intervals. Use care so that you do not cut through the side edges of the card except as shown. You must stop each snip about 1/4″ from the edge. Watch carefully to space the last cuts so that the very final cut begins from the folded edge.

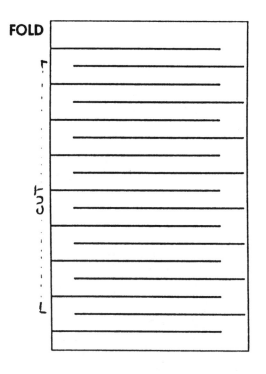

FOLD

CUT

3. Open your card. Place it on a flat surface and carefully cut along the center fold, but do not cut the fold at either end.
4. Gently stretch the ends, causing the opening to spread wider and wider. Place it over your head! You have slipped your head through a 5″ x 7″ index card! If you desire to pull the card over your shoulders and down to your feet and to step out of it, you must make your cuts closer together.

Paper-Clip Necklaces

In the early years of our country, the Indians made necklaces from beads and feathers. They used the necklaces to trade or barter for other items that they needed. You can make your own necklace to give away or to wear.

Did you think that paper clips were used only to hold papers together? Not so. Paper clips make lovely necklaces. Metal clips or plastic colored ones can be used.

Materials Required

paper clips

Directions

1. Insert one clip into the other until you have a chain long enough to encircle your neck and to hang as long as you desire.
2. Fasten the two ends together and carefully place the necklace over your head.
3. Make necklaces of different lengths or colors or make matching bracelets and anklets. Trade with your friends just as the Indians did in days of old.

Popcorn Time

The Pilgrims, some of America's early white settlers, were introduced to popcorn by the Indians. The Indians had long cultivated corn not only for popping but for other uses as well. Corn itself is an essential in our lives, with uses ranging from cereals at breakfast to being served on or off the cob as a vegetable for dinner. We can find cornstarch, corn sugar, corn oil, and corn meal and many more uses. Chickens, pigs, and cattle thrive on forms of corn.

Years ago, the pioneers stuffed their mattresses with corn husks and used them to make baskets and floor mats. Children played with dolls made from corn husks. Colonists paid their taxes with corn. At their town meetings, a kernel of corn was used to designate a "yes" vote, while a bean signified a "no" vote.

Popped corn has become a traditional treat for Americans of all ages. It is delicious served with butter or margarine and a shake or two of table salt or finely grated cheese. As children mature, many enjoy transforming the popped corn into popcorn balls, using molasses or corn syrup.

In our modern world, it is easy to have popcorn, either by using an electric popcorn popper, a cooking utensil with a tight-fitting lid, the microwave oven, or with a long-handled camping-type popper specifically designed for use over campfires.

Autumn is an appropriate time for some corn. Explain the significance of corn in the history and growth of our country and its many uses in our daily diet and eating habits.

Totem Poles

Materials Required

12" empty tube from paper towels
markers
paste
construction paper
scissors

Directions

1. Decorate a piece of construction paper with Indian designs.
2. Placing the paper lengthwise, wrap this decorated piece around the empty tube.
3. Paste the overlap together. There will be approximately 1" of uncovered tubing at the base.

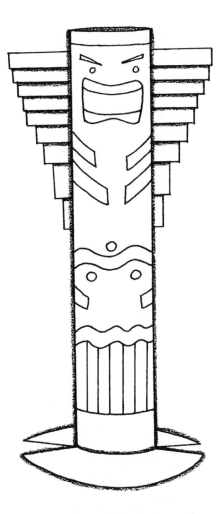

4. Cut a strip of green construction paper 3″ wide. Paste this around the bottom of the tube, leaving 2″ extended out beyond the tube. With the scissors snip this piece from its edge to the edge of the tube. Fold these pieces out. These are extra supports for the totem pole.

5. Totem poles were made by Indians of the Pacific Northwest and recorded family or tribal history. Draw simple pictures or symbols of your own family history or members and glue to the totem pole to decorate it.

Turkeys

While Mom is busy preparing the turkey for the oven, her helper can be busy drawing turkey prints.

Materials Required

brown tempera or finger paint
white construction or art paper
paper plate
crayons

Directions

1. Pour paint in a paper plate
2. Place a few sheets of the paper on the working space.
3. With the child's fingers spread apart, press the open hand into the paint.
4. With the palm and fingers well coated with paint, "stamp" the hand onto the sheets of paper.
5. The hand print creates the body of the turkey.
6. Wipe the hand clean.
7. With crayons draw an eye, beak, and red wattle on the thumb portion of the print.
8. Color the fingers as feathers.
9. Add legs and feet.

December

Christmas

Christmas is the celebration of the birth of Jesus Christ. He was born in a manger in the town of Bethlehem almost two thousand years ago. In early England a *Cristes messe* (Christ's mass) and festival were held. The celebration included a Yule log, carols, wassail bowls, decorations, gifts, and carols. The very first Christmas carol was the one sung by the angels over the fields of Bethlehem when Jesus was born. In the Gospel of Luke we learn the words that they sang: "Glory to God in the highest, and on earth peace, good will toward men." Gift giving was established by the Wise Men as they came from the East bearing gifts of gold, frankincense, and myrrh.

The tradition of displaying manger scenes began in 1223 when St. Francis of Assisi created one in the village of Greccio, Italy. Although the date of Jesus' birth is not known, Christmas came to be celebrated at the time of the winter solstice. In northern countries that is the time of snow and other winter decorations now associated with Christmas.

Dancing Snowballs

Materials Required

tall clear-glass vase
wintery scene or figure
water
mothballs
white vinegar
baking soda
measuring spoon

Directions

1. Place the wintertime figure—snowman, sled, tree—in the bottom of the vase. It should be heavy enough to stay there, or use some floral putty to affix it.
2. Pour 1/2 cup white vinegar in the vase.
3. Carefully fill the vase almost to the top with water.
4. Add several mothballs.
5. When you desire the "snowballs" to dance, add 3 tablespoons of baking soda. Watch the effervescence. The bubbles will cling to the mothballs, with the result that the "snowballs" will gracefully float up and down for a time.

Gingerbread Time

The aroma of gingerbread baking in the oven and the fragrance of ginger, molasses, cinnamon, and cloves permeating the air stir nostalgic memories of pleasant visits to Grandma's house.

Materials Required

brown grocery bag or tan construction paper or tan felt
pieces of ribbon, yarn, ricrac, lace
buttons, sequins
cotton
scissors
glue
Gingerbread made according to directions on the box to
cut with cookie cutter in the shape of gingerbread people,
or serve as a cake with whipped-cream topping
use your own favorite recipe

Directions

1. Draw a gingerbread boy and girl on an opened brown grocery bag or construction paper or on a piece of tan felt.
2. Decorate by gluing on sequins or beads for eyes, buttons for mouth. Use ricrac or ribbon as a bow.
3. To create a gingerbread boy or girl ornament for your Christmas tree, cut a double piece of brown material or paper. Tuck some cotton balls between the two layers before gluing the edges together.
4. Read aloud the story of "The Little Gingerbread Boy" while enjoying some warm gingerbread fresh from your oven.

Grapefruit Bird Feeder

I eat my yellow grapefruit
And it squirts and squirts and squirts,
And sometimes flies into my eyes
And hurts and hurts and hurts!
I wish it would keep its sticky stuff
Right in its own insides,
Instead of squirting it about
And hurting me besides!

—Author Unknown

It's always fun to learn a new use for a familiar item.

Materials Required

1/2 grapefruit
nail or pointed object
24″ piece of string
peanut butter

Directions

1. Enjoy eating the grapefruit sections. Grapefruit is great with a little honey or brown sugar sprinkled on top. After you have eaten the fruity segments, save the rind.
2. With the nail poke three or four well-spaced holes around the edge, but down far enough from the edge so that you have a threadable hole.
3. Insert the string. Allow enough length so that you will be able to hang it on a tree outside.
4. Spread peanut butter or place bread crumbs or bird seed in the grapefruit half. The hungry and cold birds will be delighted when you hang this feeder in the tree.

Paper Chain

How long a paper chain can you make? Long enough to go around the Christmas tree? Long enough to decorate a window? Long enough to reach from one end of the room to the other? Longer than you are tall? Try it.

Materials Required

red and green construction paper, or colorful pages from
an old magazine
paste
scissors
working paper or cloth to help in the cleanup

Directions

1. Cut strips a length of your choice, either uniform in size or in varying lengths and widths. Just make sure the strips are long enough to create a circle through which you can pass the next strip.
2. Extend one end of a strip over the other end and paste together.
3. Pass the next strip through the first loop and paste its ends together. Your chain has started. How far can you go with it?

Paper Lanterns

Originally, lanterns were used to protect candles from being accidentally blown out or tipped over. The Romans used lanterns with sides of thin horn to shield their oil lamps. There are many kinds of lanterns—brass, tin, fabric, clay, and glass. Campers often use a kerosene lantern as a source of light. Today make some paper lanterns, but use them only as decorations.

Materials Required

8-1/2″ x 11″ piece of construction paper
additional paper
scissors
paste

Directions

1. Fold the sheet of paper in half lengthwise and crease firmly.
2. Place the scissors at the crease and make 3" deep cuts 1" apart. Make the last cut all the way through, creating a strip 1" x 8-1/2".
3. Paste the 8-1/2" ends of the creased sheet together, forming a tube.
4. Paste the narrow strip on the top to create a handle. Your paper lantern is complete.
5. You can use the pattern to create smaller, multicolored versions for use as ornaments on the Christmas tree.

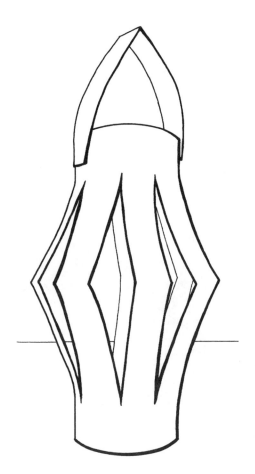

Paper Snowflakes

Earlier we learned about crystals. Snowflakes are crystals, too. If you look closely, you can see the crystalline formations. Because crystals form randomly and uniquely, it is true that no two snowflakes are identical.

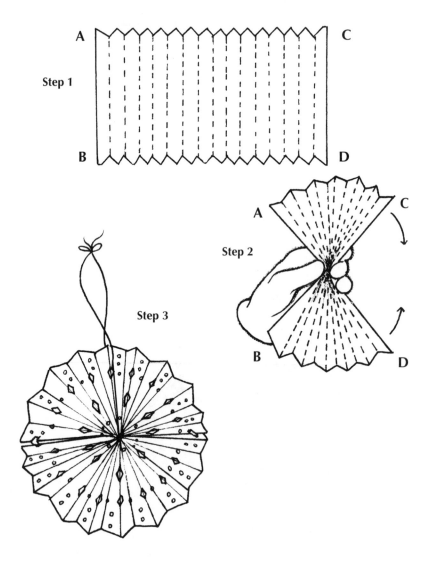

Materials Required

sheets of white paper, 8-1/2" x 11"
scissors
tape
paper punch
string or yarn

Directions

1. Fold the 8-1/2" x 11" sheet of paper in half lengthwise. Cut the paper so you now have 2 pieces each 4-1/4" x 11".
2. Accordion pleat the 11" length of paper. Cut through the folds or pleats at various intervals. Do this on left and right edge of pleats.
3. While paper is still folded, punch a hole in the center through all folds. Insert one end of the string through the hole and tie securely.
4. Tape the end sides together, A to B and C to D. Open and admire your beautiful snowflake. This is one snowflake that will not get your hands cold.
5. Another way of making a beautiful snowflake is to fold the square sheet of white paper into fourths, scallop the edges, snip pieces off at various intervals, and open.

Turtle Paperweight

Any time is a good time to make and give gifts. This month is an especially good time to start assembling gifts to have on hand for those special events and celebrations that will soon be here. Remember those stones you gathered back in summer? Now is the time to use them in making a gift.

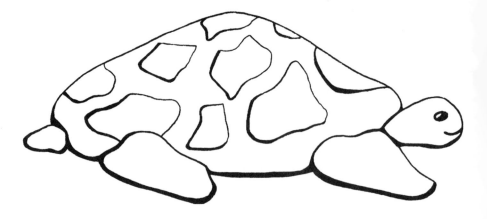

Materials Required

an oval-shaped stone, approximately 4″ long,
flat on one side and rounded on the other
6 small stones, 4 close to the same size for the feet
a smaller stone for the head and
one still smaller for the tail
markers
Sobo glue

Directions

1. On the rounded side of the larger stone, with a dark brown marker, draw markings such as you find on the shells of turtles. After these dry, color them in with either green or yellow.
2. Place the four stones in proper position for the feet and carefully glue them into place on the large stone. After these dry, glue in place the head and the tail.
3. After these are dry, use the black marker and create lines on the feet and eyes on the head. You now have a very useful paperweight, a gift that anyone of any age will be delighted to receive.

Spool Ornaments

It's always fun to decorate the Christmas tree with pretty ornaments. It's even more fun if you make the ornaments yourself. Here's how.

Materials Required

empty spools
paints
(depending on age of child: water, spray enamel, markers)
beads, pearls, sequins
narrow ribbon or plastic strips or ricrac
glue
scissors
small paintbrush
newspaper or work cloth

Directions

1. Spread the newspaper or work cloth at the table. Remove the labels from the ends of the spools.
2. Color or paint the spools.
3. Add beads and sequins. If you use enamel paint, it also serves as an adhesive. If you use markers or water paints, wait until the spools dry completely and then spread a few drops of glue wherever you wish to attach a bead or sequin.
4. Thread the narrow strips of ribbon or lace through the holes of the spools and make a secure knot or bow. The ornament is ready to be given as a gift or to hang on your own tree.

How-to Hints

There are many craft recipes that can be made at home with adult supervision. The list of possibilities is endless. It is innovative, economical, and fun to prepare craft recipes in your own kitchen. With "a little of this" and "a little of that" blended and stirred together, you'll be surprised at what you can create.

Circle from a Square
Salt-and-Flour Clay
Play Clay
Easy-to-Make Paste
Glue from Milk
Home-Style Finger Paint
Ink for Transfers
Basket Pattern
Place Mat
Rectangle to Square
Supply Box
Extra Ideas for Fun Indoors
Constellation Maps

Circle from a Square

To create a circle from a square piece of paper, fold the square into equal fourths. Draw an arc between points A and B. Cut this portion off and you have a circle.

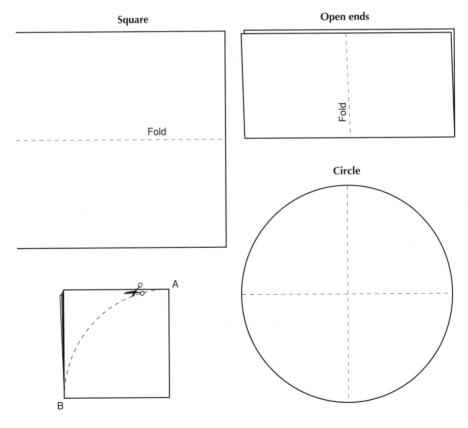

Salt-and-Flour Clay

For making ornaments and interesting figures, use the following recipe.

Ingredients Required

1-1/2 cups flour (not self-rising)
1 cup table salt
3 teaspoons alum powder (used as a preservative)
1/2 cup cold water
1 cup boiling water
2 tablespoons vegetable oil
food coloring

Directions

1. Adult supervision is needed, especially for the boiling of water.
2. Mix flour, salt, and alum powder in a large mixing bowl.
3. Add the oil and then the cold water. Add the boiling water, stirring well. Scrape the sides so that all ingredients are well mixed.
4. Add color as desired.
5. Store in containers with tight-fitting lids.
6. After being shaped into figures or ornaments, the clay can be left out to dry overnight and then painted. If you are creating an ornament or an item that you will want to hang, be sure to make a hole through which you can place a hanger or thread later.

Play Clay

Combinations of different ingredients result in various types of "play clay" or "play dough." All are fun to use for making things.

Ingredients Required

2 cups baking soda
1 cup cornstarch
1 1/4 cups cold water

Directions

1. Adult supervision is necessary.
2. Combine all ingredients in a saucepan.
3. Stir until smooth.
4. Bring to a boil and boil for one minute, stirring until mixture is consistency of mashed potatoes.
5. Pour onto a tray or cookie sheet.
6. Cover with a damp towel. Let cool.
7. Knead before using.
8. Store in airtight plastic containers in refrigerator. Will keep 3 months.
9. Ornaments or figures can be made from this as is and then decorated or painted. The play clay can also be divided into separate containers with a few drops of different food colors added.
10. Permit the ornaments or figures to harden by leaving unwrapped overnight. If making ornaments to hang, always remember to pierce a small hole for hanging before letting the objects harden.

Easy-to-Make Paste

Ingredients Required

1/4 cup wheat flour (not self-rising)
1/2 teaspoon alum powder
1/4 cup sugar
1-3/4 cups water
1/4 teaspoon oil of wintergreen or oil of cloves

Directions

1. Into a medium-sized saucepan place the dry ingredients: flour, sugar, and alum powder. Adult supervision is required.
2. Slowly add the water a little at a time to avoid lumping. Place on a low burner and bring to a boil.
3. Continue until mixture has thickened and becomes clear in color. You must "watch this pot." It will boil but requires your constant attention to prevent sticking. Remove from stove. Cool slightly.
4. Add the oil of wintergreen or the oil of cloves.
5. This is a thinner paste and can be used effectively in paper maché or when pasting pictures on posters or in scrapbooks.
6. Store in a jar with screw-type lid.

Glue from Milk

You're ready to work on a project that requires gluing pieces of paper together and you discover that you have no glue. Relax. Perhaps you have some on hand and don't realize it. Look in your refrigerator. Yes, that's right, the refrigerator, and then the pantry shelf. Make some yourself.

Ingredients and Materials Required

2 cups skim milk
6 tablespoons vinegar
1 tablespoon sodium bicarbonate (baking soda)
1/4 cup water
enameled saucepan or heat-proof glass pan
stirring spoon
quart or pint measuring cup
an unbreakable bowl
a strainer
small container with lid for storing the glue

Directions

1. Stove use is required. A parent or adult must be present for this activity.
2. Pour the two cups of skim milk into the saucepan. Add the six tablespoons of vinegar. Place the pan on a burner and heat slowly, stirring carefully as the ingredients warm.
3. While stirring, notice the milk curdle and separate into small lumps or curds. As soon as this starts to happen, remove the pan from the heat and place on a safe, unheated area. Continue to stir until the curdling stops.
4. Pour this mixture into the measuring container that you used previously. Remember "Little Miss Muffet sat on a tuffet, eating her curds and whey." You are not going to eat your experiment, but you have made curds (the lumps) and whey (the liquid) of your own. Don't sit on a tuffet either because you still have work to do.
5. Use the strainer and pour the curds and whey into it. Place the curds into the container to be used to store your finished product.
6. Add 1/4 cup water to the curds along with 1 tablespoon sodium bicarbonate (baking soda). Notice the little bubbles that form. This happens because of the reaction between the sodium bicarbonate and the vinegar still present in the curds. Your glue is now ready for use.
7. As the children mature, you may want to explain "scientifically" the reactions and terms *acid, lactic acid, casein.*

Home-Style Finger Paint

Materials Required

1/4 cup dry laundry starch
1/4 cup cold water
1-1/2 cups boiling water
1/2 cup mild soap flakes
food colors
1 tablespoon glycerin *or* the following:
2 tablespoons unscented talcum powder and
1/4 teaspoon boric acid solution

Directions

1. Place the starch in a saucepan. Gradually add the cold water to dissolve the starch. Adult supervision is required.
2. Add the hot water slowly and stir as you do. Cook the mixture over low heat until it bubbles and is clear in color.
3. Add the soap flakes and continue to stir. When cooled add the glycerin (or the talcum powder and boric acid solution).
4. Divide into empty, clean plastic margarine tubs and add drops of food coloring until the desired shades are achieved.

Ink for Transfers

If you see an interesting comic strip character and would love to reproduce it for the sheer fun of it, try making the following.

Materials Required

2 tablespoons mild soap flakes
1/4 cup very hot water
1 tablespoon turpentine
a small watercolor brush
pictures desired for transferring
paper, stationery, or sweatshirt

Directions

1. Requires adult supervision.
2. Add the soap flakes to the water. Stir.
3. Gradually add the turpentine. Store this solution in a jar with a screw-top lid for safekeeping.
4. To transfer a picture, dip the brush into the solution and "paint" over the picture to be transferred.
5. Wait about 15 seconds. Place the piece of paper or material to which you want to transfer the picture over the original. Use the

outer curved surface of a tablespoon to gently rub over the area to receive the transfer.

6. Children can have fun transferring comic strips or portions of a magazine picture. Some magazine pages and glossy surfaces require extra solution. There is no limit to what the uses are: greeting cards, stationery, designs on clothing, and much more.

7. The transfer ink stores well in a tightly closed jar. If the solution should harden, place the jar in a bowl filled with warm water for 15 minutes or until solution returns to a liquid state.

Basket Pattern

To create a basket, take a square piece of paper. Fold it into thirds in one direction. Crease these lines. Now fold into thirds in the other direction. Crease. You can now see 9 small squares or sections. Cut on the designated lines, fold respective sides up, and paste the sides together. This will create a deep but small basket.

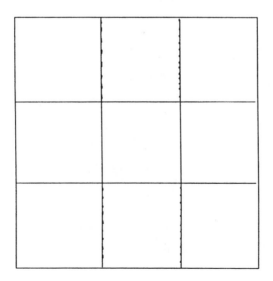

To adjust the depth of a basket, fold the squared piece of paper into half and then fourths. Turn the paper and again fold so that large square has been creased into 16 small ones. Cut on designated lines and continue.

Place Mat

Create a pattern for your "helper" to follow when he or she is assisting you at mealtime.

Materials Required

a paper place mat or sturdy piece of paper, 12" x 18"
pictures from an old magazine
markers or paper plate and plastic utensils
paste

Directions

1. From an old magazine cut pictures of a plate, glass, knife, fork, spoon, napkin, or use inexpensive paper and plastic ones.
2. Paste the items on the place mat as a pattern for little ones to learn how to set the table and use as a guide when helping.

Rectangle to Square

If instructions call for a square piece of paper and you have only rectangular shaped ones, here's how to transform the rectangular piece into a square.

Directions

1. Measure the width of the paper.
2. Measure this amount along the length.
3. Mark it and fold the remaining portion down. Trim off the extra inches.
4. You now have a square piece of paper and are ready to continue with your work.

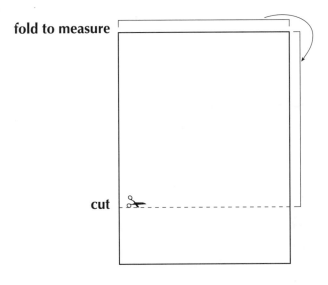

fold to measure

cut

Supply Box

Tell your children the story of Pandora who had a box which she was not to open. But you can have a box that you should open and often.

Materials Required

a box with four sides, bottom, lid, and large enough
to serve as a storage container for your craft items
markers
supplies

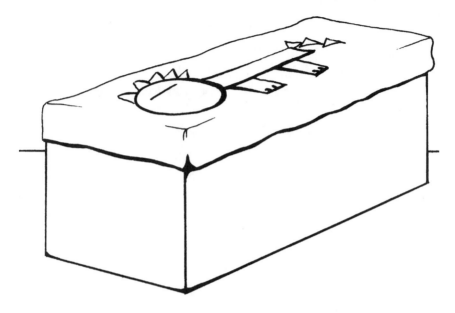

Directions

1. Decorate your box in any manner that is appealing to you.
2. Place construction paper, paste, yarn, scraps of material, felt, markers, crayons, and craft supplies inside so that they are always handy and cleanup time is easy.

Extra Ideas for Fun Indoors

Rain, rain go away,
Come again another day.
Someone here
Wants to play!

—Folk Rhyme

Even if it's pouring down rain or too cold or too hot to have fun outdoors, there are plenty of alternatives for having fun indoors.

1. When it's cold or rainy outside, spread a blanket, sheet, or table-cloth on the floor and serve silly sandwiches "picnic style" indoors.
2. Play grocery store. Use empty boxes that you have saved or "shop" in your pantry. Do you have a scale handy for weighing?
3. Draw a picture of the family. Did the youngster remember each person and each pet?
4. Organize family photographs or look at albums of the family and do a "remember when" time. Look at the albums of the children when they were babies. Reminisce about specific events and happenings.
5. Watch from a window and count the cars. How many red ones went by, how many blue, green?
6. Have the helper "clean" the sink. A spray bottle containing some water with a few drops of vinegar makes a wonderful cleaning agent.
7. Play beauty or barber shop. Get the brush, comb, manicure set, mirror. Arrange an appointment time and welcome your next "customer."
8. Hide an object in one of the rooms. As the seeker hunts, announce "You're getting warm" or "warmer" or "cold" as dictated by the nearness of the seeker to the hidden object.
9. Introduce a magnifying glass and a magnet to your child. Demonstrate the fun and the valuable aspects of each. Examine different items under the magnifying glass. Experiment with the degree of attraction between various types of objects and the magnet.
10. Play some music. What is the best way to move to it: march, skip, hop, slide? Quickly or slowly?
11. Pour lemonade into paper cups. Place cups in the freezer until lemonade is partially frozen. Eat with a spoon.
12. Play a game of Rhythm Claps, Mazoo, Hokey Pokey, Simon Says, or Here We Go 'Round the Mulberry Bush.
13. Cut pictures from an old magazine and create an alphabet book. Work together to find pictures of objects beginning with A—apple; B—baby; C—corn, and so forth. The fun is working together to locate, cut, paste, and create a book.
14. Create a "lap desk" by using a cardboard box and cutting two "tunnels" to accommodate the legs. This is also useful for "desk work" when a youngster must remain in bed.

15. Create your own dot-to-dot pictures, mazes, and lacing cards.
16. Use a piece of wrapping paper or butcher paper longer than the child is tall. Place it on the floor. Have the child stretch out on the paper. Trace around him or her and form an outline of the body. Have the child fill in eyes, ears, nose, mouth, hair, fingers, feet, etc. Print his or her name on the paper.
17. Place several items that are available around the house into an empty shoe box. Include a variety of things: a funnel, measuring cups, plastic containers, string, crayons, paper, etc. Challenge the young ones to "invent" a game or "new product."
18. Use any cardboard box of appropriate size, with either a hinged top or a separate lid that fits securely so that contents will not spill out. Cover any advertising on the box with contact paper, extra wallpaper, or wrapping paper. Decorate by gluing some odd buttons onto the lid. You have created a button box—a great gift for that certain someone on your gift list.
19. Create a box for saving "dress ups" or costumes.
20. Discuss "what if" situations: What if no one was home one day; what if a stranger offered a ride; what if a billfold with money was found; what if a schoolmate did something very wrong?

Constellation Maps

The Big Dipper (Ursa Major)

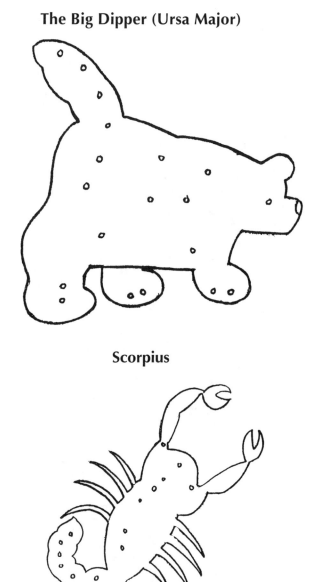

Scorpius

Leo

Orion

Index